THE WORKS OF
GEORGE BORROW

EDITED, WITH MUCH HITHERTO
UNPUBLISHED MANUSCRIPT, BY

CLEMENT SHORTER

NORWICH EDITION

VOLUME IX

GEORGE BORROW

THE SONGS OF SCANDINAVIA

AND OTHER POEMS AND BALLADS

VOLUME III

AMS PRESS INC. • New York • 1967

Reprinted with the permission
of the original publisher

AMS PRESS, INC.
New York, N.Y. 10003

Manufactured in the U.S.A.

CONTENTS OF VOL. III

SONGS FROM THE GERMAN (*continued*)

SONG FROM THE DUTCH

SONG FROM THE BASQUE

SONGS OF FRANCE

THE SONGS OF SCANDINAVIA

SONGS OF SPAIN

SONGS OF PORTUGAL

SONGS OF ITALY

SONGS OF ANCIENT GREECE AND ROME

CONTENTS

SONGS OF POLAND AND RUSSIA

SONGS OF HUNGARY

SONGS OF MODERN GREECE

GYPSY SONGS

THE SONGS OF SCANDINAVIA

SONGS OF THE EAST

CONTENTS

MISCELLANEOUS

THE SONGS OF SCANDINAVIA

CONTENTS

APPENDIX

ROMANTIC BALLADS AND MISCELLANEOUS PIECES

ROMANTIC BALLADS

MISCELLANIES

THE SONGS OF SCANDINAVIA

THE DIVER

‘ **Where** is the man who will dive for his King,
  In the pool as it rushes with turbulent sweep ?
A cup from this surf-beaten jetty I fling,
  And he who will seek it below in the deep,
And will bring it again to the light of the day,
As the meed of his valour shall bear it away.

‘ Now courage, my knights, and my warriors bold,
  For, one, two, and three, and away it shall go—’
He toss’d, as he said it, the goblet of gold
  Deep, deep in the howling abysses below.—
‘ Where is the hero who ventures to brave
The whirl of the pool, and the break of the wave ? ’

The steel-coated lancemen, and nobles around,
  Spoke not, but they trembled in silent surprise,
And pale they all stood on the cliff’s giddy bound,
  And no one would venture to dive for the prize.
‘ Three times have I spoke, but no hero will spring
And dive for the goblet, and dive for the King.’

But still they were silent and pale as before,
  Till a brave son of Eirin, in venturous pride,
Dash’d forth from the lancemen’s trembling corps
  And canted his helm, cast his mantle aside,
While spearman, and noble, and lady, and knight,
Gazed on the bold stripling in breathless affright

Unmoved by the thoughts of his horrible doom,
He mounted the cliff—and he paus'd on his leap,
For the waves which the pool had imbibed in its womb
Were spouted in thunder again from the deep,—
Yes ! as they return'd, their report was as loud
As the peal when it bursts from the storm-riven cloud.

It roared and it drizzled, it hiss'd and it whirl'd,
And it bubbled like water when mingled with flame,
And columns of foam to the heaven were hurl'd,
And billow on billow tumultuously came ;
It seem'd that the womb of the ocean would bear
Sea over sea to the uppermost air.

It thundered again as the wave gather'd slow,
And black from the drizzling foam as it fell,
The mouth of the fathomless tunnel below
Was seen like the pass to the regions of hell ;
The waters roll round it, and gather and boom,
And then all at once disappear in the gloom.

And now ere the waves had returned from the deep,
The youth wiped the sweat-drops which hung on his brows,
And he plunged—and the cataracts over him sweep,
And a shout from his terrified comrades arose ;
And then there succeeded a horrible pause,
For the whirlpool had clos'd its mysterious jaws.

And stiller it grew on the watery waste,
  In the womb of the ocean it bellow'd alone,
The knights said their Aves in terrified haste,
  And crowded each pinnacle, jetty, and stone:
'The high-hearted stripling is whelm'd in the tide,
Ah! wail him,' was echoed from every side.

'If the monarch had buried his crown in the pool
  And said: "He shall wear it who brings it again,"
I would not have been so insensate a fool
  As to dive when all hope of returning were vain;
What heaven conceals in the gulfs of the deep,
Lies buried for ever, and there it must sleep.'

Full many a burden the whirlpool had borne,
  And spouted it forth on the drizzling surge,
But nought but a mast that was splinter'd and torn,
  Or the hull of a vessel was seen to emerge;
But wider and wider it opens its jaws,
And louder it gurgles, and louder it draws.

It drizzled, it thunder'd, it hiss'd, and it whirl'd,
  And it bubbled like water when mingled with flame,
And columns of foam to the heaven were hurl'd,
  And flood upon flood from the deep tunnel came;
And then with a noise like the storm from the north,
The hellish eruption was vomited forth.

But ah ! what is that on the wave's foamy brim,
  Disgorged with an ocean of wreck and of wood ?
'Tis the snow-white arm and the shoulder of him
  Who daringly dived for the glittering meed :
'Tis he, 'tis the stripling so hardy and bold,
Who swings in his left hand the goblet of gold.

He draws a long breath as the breaker he leaves,
  Then swims through the water with many a strain,
While all his companions exultingly heave
  Their voices above the wild din of the main :
' 'Tis he, O! 'tis he, from the horrible hole
The brave one has rescued his body and soul.'

He reach'd the tall jetty, and kneeling he laid
  The massy gold goblet in triumph and pride
At the foot of the monarch, who instantly made
  A sign to his daughter who stood by his side :
She fill'd it with wine, and the youth with a spring
Receiv'd it, and quaff'd it, and turn'd to the King.

' Long life to the monarch ! how happy are they
Who breathe and exist in the sun's rosy light,
But he who is doom'd in the ocean to stray,
  Views nothing around him but horror and night;
Let no one henceforward be tempted like me
To pry in the secrets contain'd in the sea.

' I felt myself seized, with the quickness of thought
  The whirlpool entomb'd me in body and limb,
And billow on billow tumultuously brought
  Its cataracts o'er me ; in vain did I swim,
For like a mere pebble with horrible sound
The force of the double stream twisted me round.

'But God in His mercy, for to Him alone
  In the moment of danger I ever have clung,
Did bear me towards a projection of stone :
  I seized it in transport, and round it I hung;
The goblet lay too on a corally ledge,
  Which jutted just over the cataract's edge.

'And then I look'd downward, and horribly deep
  And twinkling sheen in the darkness below,
And though to the hearing it ever might sleep,
  Yet still the eye clouded with terror might know,
That serpents and creatures that made my blood cool,
Were swimming and splashing about in the pool.

'Ball'd up to a mass, in a moment uncoil'd,
  They rose, and again disappear'd in the dark,
And down in the billows which over them boil'd
  I saw a behemoth contend with a shark ;
The sounds of their hideous duel awaken
The black-bellied whale, and the slumbering craken.

'Still, still did I linger forlorn, and oppress'd
  With a feeling of terror that curdled my blood;
Ah ! think of a human and sensible breast
  Enclosed with the hideous shapes of the flood ;
Still, still did I linger, but far from the reach
Of those that I knew would await on the beach.

'Methought that a serpent towards me did creep,
And trailing behind him whole fathoms of length,
He open'd his jaws ; and I dropp'd from the steep
Round which I had clung with expiring strength :
'Twas well that I did so, the stream bore me up,
And here is thy servant, and there is the cup.'

He then was retiring, a look from the King
Detain'd him : ' My hero, the cup is thine own,
'Tis richly thy meed, but I 'll give thee this ring,
Beset with a diamond and chrysolite stone,
If again thou wilt dive, and discover to me
What 's hid in the deepest abyss of the sea.'

The daughter heard that with compassionate thought,
Quick, quick to the feet of the monarch she flew :
' O father, desist from this horrible sport,
He has done what no other would venture to do,
If the life of a creature thou fain must destroy,
Let a noble take place of this generous boy.'

The monarch has taken the cup in his hand,
And tumbled it down in the bellowing sea :
' And if thou canst bring it again to the strand,
The first, and the best of my knights thou shalt be ;
If that will not tempt thee, this maid thou shalt wed,
And share as a husband the joys of her bed.'

Then the pride of old Eirin arose in his look,
 And it flash'd from his eye-balls courageously keen,
One glance on the beautiful vision he took,
 And he saw her change colour, and sink on the green.
' By the stool of Saint Peter the prize I 'll obtain,'
He shouted, and instantly dived in the main.

The waters sunk down, and a thundering peal
 Announced that the time of their sojourn was o'er ;
Each eye is cast downward in terrified zeal,
 As forth from the tunnel the cataracts pour.
The waters rush up, and the waters subside ;
But ah ! the bold diver remains in the tide.

MOUNTAIN SONG

THAT pathway before ye, so narrow and gray,
  To the depths of the chasm is leading;
But giants stand sentinel over the way,
  And threaten death to the unheeding:
Be silent and watchful, each step that you take,
Lest the sound of your voices the lions [1] awake.

And there is a bridge—see yonder its span
  O'er the gush of the cataract bending,
It never receiv'd its foundation from man,—
  Each mortal would die in ascending:
The torrents, uprooting the pine and the larch,
Dash over, but never can splinter its arch.

And now we must enter a hidden ravine,
  With its crags loosely tottering o'er us;
Pass on, and a valley delightfully green
  Will open its bosom before us.
O! that I could fly from each worldly alloy,
To finish my days in its circle of joy.

Down from a cave four rivers are hurl'd,
  Each musters its force like a legion;
And then they seek all the four parts of the world,
  Each choosing a separate region:
All from the cavern are secretly tost,
They murmur away, and for ever are lost.

[1] The avalanches, called in the Swiss dialect *lawine,* or lions.

Three pinnacles tower, and enter the blue
High over the mountains and waters ;
There wanton, surrounded by vapour and dew,
The bands of the heavenly daughters ;
And there they continue their desolate reign,
Their charms are unseen, and are wished for in vain.

The queen of the regions sits high on her throne,
And our sages have told me in story,
That she wears on her temples a chrysolite crown,
Which causes yon halo of glory ;
The sun on her robes darts his arrows of gold,
And brightens them only—they ever are cold.

THRESHING SONG

YE Youths and ye Maidens, hark, Chanticleer cries,
  Wake up,
And Morning so gloriously tingeth the skies,
  Wake up.
The Neighbours are threshing all round about here,
Clap, clip, clap, salutes from each quarter the ear,
No true mettled youth and no maiden
Will doze any longer their bed in.
    Clap, clip, clop,
    Clop, clip, clap.

Ye Youths and ye Maidens, hark, Chanticleer cries,
  Wake up,
And Morning so gloriously tingeth the skies,
  Wake up.
God prospers our labour extremely this year,
The sheaves are long, heavy 's the blessing they bear,
The beans, and what 's better the barley,
O, I trow it will bushel up rarely.
    Clap, clip, clop,
    Clop, clip, clap.

Ye Youths and ye Maidens, hark, Chanticleer cries,
Wake up,
And Morning so gloriously tingeth the skies,
Wake up.
The Grandmother brushes the oven clean out,
Fresh blows the wind, whirling the mill sails about,
When we 've thresh'd we 'll to grinding betake us,
That she new bread to-morrow may bake us.
Clap, clip, clop,
Clop, clip, clap.

CHORUS OF THE NUNS OF SANTA CLARA

O Christmas night, O Christmas night,
But ill can Herod bear the light
  Illumining thy gloom profound,
A light that 's worshipp'd far and near;
No supplication he will hear
  However piercing it may sound.

By taking harmless infants' lives,
To slay the Saviour child he strives
  And wakes in town and land a shriek,
In Bethlehem and on the wold,
And makes the soul of Rachel bold,
  Who wandering goes her babes to seek.

Now looks she east, now looks she west,
Ah! who shall soothe her heart distrest,
  When she beholds her children dead?
She sees them lying in their gore,
The beauteous babes she lately bore,
  And many a warrior's faulchion red.

The milk she sees upon the tips
Of her dear infants' pallid lips,
  From mother's paps but freshly drain'd;
She sees the tender tear-drops too
Hanging upon their cheeks like dew,
  But all, alas! with blood bestain'd.

The eyebrows now are arching o'er
Sweet little laughing orbs no more,
Which caus'd the mother heart to leap ;
Those orbs are stiff, their motion fled,
A heaven the countenance which made,
Before a mist did o'er it sweep.

O, who can all the woe declare
Or say how many flowrets fair
Were wither'd there and left forlorn,
Ere they their tender leaves unbound
Or cast their sweet perfume around
Or drank the first mead of the morn ?

So lays the steel the corn ears low,
So strews the gust when tempests blow
The foliage of the greenwood tree.
O, who can tyrant's wrath assuage,
When dark suspicion bids it rage ?
What note can soothe it one degree ?

Distracted Rachel, cease to cry,
Thy babes the death of martyrs die.
They 're first fruits of that seed of joy,
Which from thy blood begins to spring,
Shall bloom in honor of heaven's ring,
And which no tyrant shall destroy.

THE WELL-STEWED PIGEON

If in heaven's halls of state
Folks on pigeons ever dine,
They ne'er tasted one more fine
Than the one this day I ate ;
O, its savoury smell was great,
Such as well might tempt, I trow,
One that 's dead to lift his brow :
O, I 'm sure the heavenly legions
Would rejoice to eat such pigeons,
Could they hunger ever know.

THE EVE OF HASTINGS

THE night before the dreadful day,
The night before, as I 've heard say,
The Englishmen were nothing sad,
Laughing all as were they mad,
Drinking till their cheeks were red,
None that night lay down on bed.
I would you had seen the throng,
How they stamped and danced and sung ;
' Bublie,' they cried and ' Wassail,'
' Pass the can ' and ' Drink hale,'
' Drink abuck,' ' Drink about,'
' Drink success ' and ' Drink out.'
Merry were the Englishmen,
But not so the Norman men.
All the night they prayers said,
Beat their breasts and tears shed,
Told the priests with grievous moan
Of the crimes that they had done.
He who could not find a priest
To his comrade him confessed.

And as the ensuing fray
Should be fought on Saturday,
The Normans of their own accord
Vowed a vow to God their Lord,
If they should survive the fray,
Would ne'er eat flesh upon that day.

Constantia's Bishop Geofferie
Bent with the penitents his knee,
Confessed full many a warrior brave
And many a benediction gave,
Also Oddo of Baieu,
Who on the morn showed prowess true,
Bishop high of Baessine,
Son of noble Herluine,
Brother uterine was he
Of the Duke of Normandie,
To whose aid he brought a train,
Levied from Oddo's own domain.
Happed upon the fourteenth day
Of October month the fray.

THE BATTLE

AND now a squadron they descry,
Covering the champain far and nigh ;
The famed gonfanon o'er it glowed,
The banner which the Pope bestowed.
Beside it came the Duke on horse,
Around him all his choicest force ;
There was the cavalier of pride,
The vassal and the warrior tried ;
There was the baron stern of mien,
Stout halberdier and archer keen,
Whose duty 'twas in battle strife
To guard their Duke's beloved life.
The lads and all the servant crew
Of war's grim trade who nothing knew,
Who had the baggage 'neath their care,
Turned to a hill and halted there.
The priests and men in orders they
Unto another took their way,
Arranged them on its topmost height
To pray to God and view the fight.
Harald beheld the Duke come on,
Beheld the arms which glittering shone,
And saw in masses three the foes
Who at three points to strike propose ;
He scarcely knew which most to dread,
And thus with faltering accents said :

' O, we 've been guided ill, I see,
And much I fear disgraced shall be.
The Flanders Count has me deceived ;
Fool I who such a knave believed,
For judging from the brief he sent,
Written in tone most confident,
I never thought the Duke 'gainst me
Could come with such vast chivalry ;
Therefore too long have I delayed,
Too little preparation made.
O, how my blindness now I rue.'
His brother Gurth to him he drew,
They placed them by their standard's side
And unto God for succour cried.
Their blood relations round them pressed,
The barons too who loved them best ;
They all resolve to bear them brave,
Since bravery now alone could save.
Each warrior stands in haubert cased,
The shield at neck, the sword at waist ;
Great hatchets at their necks they bore,
Which oft had severed necks of yore.
On foot they stood in firm array,
Dauntless their bearing, I must say ;
But if the future they had known,
They might have raised a dismal groan.
For well might English hearts dismay
The issue of that dreadful day.
' Holy crosse ' they often cry
And ' Godamighty ' frequently :
In English ' Holycrosse ' doth mean
What ' Sainte Croi ' doth in French, I ween.

Whilst 'Godamighty' answers all
To 'Deu tot poissant,' our call.
The Normans three divisions form;
From three directions they would storm;
That they came on in parties three
All writers that I 've read agree.
The first and second came on fast,
Then came the strongest band and last,
The great Duke and his retinue:
In gallant fashion on they drew;
When the two hosts each other spied,
Rose tumult wild from either side.
O, would you 'd heard the buccines blown,
The blast of grails, the trumpet's tone,
And seen the martial ranks prepared,
The lances serried, bucklers reared,
For onslaught or defence amain,
How bows were bent and arrows ta'en.
The Englishmen maintain their place,
But onward aye the Normans pace;
Soon as they saw the Normans come,
The English raised their sullen hum;
A thrill throughout their army rushed,
Some cheeks were pallid, more were flushed;
If cowards trembled, brave men frowned;
England's host maintained its ground.

Before the Duke bold Taillefer
Upon a horse of swiftness rare
Rode chanting loud the ancient strain
Of Rowland wight and Charlemagne,
Of Oliver and good knights all,
Who fighting died at Roncesval.

And when they, ever riding on,
Nigh to the English host had won :
'Sire,' said the minstrel, 'you 're aware
That I have served you many a year
And me my service wage you owe,
I 'd gladly, sire, receive it now ;
The guerdon which I now require,
Which I with all my heart desire
Is that thou 'lt grant to me the right
Of striking first this day in fight.'
The Duke exclaimed, 'I grant it free.'
The minstrel pressed his steed with knee,
Before the rest he shouting ran
And met and killed an Englishman.
Right through the body 'neath the breast
The lance has passed he bore on rest ;
The dead man on the ground he threw
And drawing sword another slew,
Then cried to his companions 'Come !
Why stay ye there! strike home! strike home!'
Soon as they saw the second blow
Our Normans rushed upon the foe ;
Then rose a dreadful noise and roar,
From either side the people pour ;
The fiery Normans fierce attack,
The stubborn English drive them back ;
The ones they strike, the others thrust,
Full many a warrior bites the dust ;
Behold the battle now begun,
The bloodiest fought beneath the sun.
The trumpet's clang you then might hear,
The sound of fiercely driven spear,

With crash of clubs that wound so drear,
With clash of swords and soldiers, cheer;
Sometimes the Englishmen retire,
Then straight return with fury dire;
Sometimes the Normans swift come on
And back again as swift are gone.
'God aide, God aide,' the Normans shout,
'Out,' the English answer, 'Out.'
Then you would see 'twixt knights on high,
English and Norman infantry,
Artful feints and fearful shocks,
Thrusts of lances, faulchion strokes;
The Normans shout when English die,
Insulting words so plenteous fly,
Each other oft they do defy,
But neither knows the other's cry,
Normans swear the English bark,
Because their words to them are dark.
Hotter still the conflict grows,
Blood more free than water flows.
These succumb and those prevail,
Brave men hew and cowards quail;
Good are Normans to attack,
The English to repel not slack,
Blows are taken, blows are given,
Corselets pierced and bucklers riven;
These retreat and these advance,
'Tis now with England, now with France.

Amidst the plain, behind the French,
There yawned a deep and murky trench;
They 'd passed it coming on with speed,
And of it taken little heed.

The Englishmen, you now must know,
Had charged and pushed the Normans so,
They 'd forced them to its steepy side ;
Sudden adown it, terrified,
Falling by hundreds, men are spied,
Horsemen and the good steeds they ride.
They rolled, they gasped, in vain they tried
To rise within that trench, they died.
Therein of English fell no few,
Whom down with them the Normans drew.
Died not in all the battle's course
So many of the Norman force,
As in that horrid trench's hold,
As men assert the dead who told.
The valets who, apart from war,
Stood with the baggage 'neath their care,
Would gladly have abandoned all,
When they beheld the Frenchmen fall
Into that fatal trench's womb,
From whence they never more could come ;
O, they were filled with mighty dread
And gladly, gladly would have fled,
Leaving the baggage all alone,
Had they a place of refuge known.
When Oddo of the shaven crown,
Bishop of famed Bayeux's town,
Beheld their plight, he shouted ' Stay,
You have no cause to run away,
No cause to be the least dismayed ;
We 'll conquer yet with God's good aid.'
Then all the serving train took heart
And swore they 'd die before they 'd start.

Then Oddo galloped, spurring well
To where the battle seemed most fell,
By him good service then was done.
He has put on a habergeon,
Above the shirt so pure and white
In which his stalwart frame was dight.
Him on his courser white and tall
Straight recognised the Normans all.
Within his hand a staff he held ;
Where he the greatest need beheld,
There, there was he with words that burn ;
He made the flying Normans turn,
Oft made them charge and strike with zeal
Stout blows which caused their foes to reel.
From the ninth hour of morn that day,
When first the fight began to bray,
Till three o'clock past noon, I trow ;
'Twas now with French, with English now,
No one could say which side would stand
And which was doomed to win the land.

THE MARSEILLAISE

SONS of lovely France, arise!
  Glory's day is dawning clear,
Tyrant force before our eyes
  Dares its bloody flag to rear;
In yon plains do ye not hear
  Those ferocious soldiers roar?
  In your arms they 'd shed the gore
Of your sons and friends most dear.

To arms, brothers! form in battle array!
Away, away.
Let blood, impure blood, drench our clay.

What means those Kings combined
  Those traitors, that slavish throng?
For whom are those chains designed,
  Those fetters prepared so long?
For us? of such horrid wrong
  How the thought alone doth sting!
  Do they think they back can bring
To the bondage of old the strong?

What! shall strangers the law proclaim
  At our hearth's domestic glow?
Cohorts of hireling name
  Our fierce warriors overthrow?

Great God, shall our foreheads bow
  To the yoke chained hands upreared ?
  And foreign despots e'er . . .[1]
. . .[1] for our weal and woe.

Quake, tyrants, and you base clan,
  Whom e'en tyrants scorn and slight ;
The parricidal plan
  Ye harbour we will requite ;
All are soldiers ye to fight,
  Should our heroes fall, the field
  A fresh supply would yield,
All eager your heads to smite.

To tread the career we trust,
  When our elders are dead and cold,
We shall find their sacred dust
  And the trace of their deeds behold.
Though a . . .[1] desire we hold
  To survive than to share their tomb,
  This or that is our splendid doom
To avenge them or join their mould.

Sacred love of the native land,
  The guide of our soldiers be !
Dear freedom, unsheath thy brand,
  Fight for them who fight for thee !
To our banners may victory
  Haste, haste, at thy manly cry,
  That thy foes, as they bleed and die,
May thy triumph and our glory see !

[1] MS. illegible.

THE DEATH OF NAPOLEON

HE 's dead—O, quite as immovable,
As soon as the death sigh had been given,
Stretch'd lay the body forgetful,
Reft of so mighty a spirit.
Stricken, astounded, astonish'd
At the news the whole world stands.

Musing upon the last moments
Of the man it calleth the fateful,
It cannot conceive when a similar
Shade with the feet of a mortal
It should ever again see striding
Over the blood bedrenched sands.

Him on the gilt throne of his glory
My spirit beheld and was silent :
When, with change oft repeated,
He fell, rose again, and lay prostrate,
From mingling her own with the million
Of voices she chose to refrain.

Himself he proclaim'd and two centuries
Arm'd and array'd 'gainst each other,
Turn'd them submissive towards him,
As if from his like they awaited
Their fate ; he silence commandeth
And betwixt them as arbiter sate.

He vanish'd and in narrow limits
Spent his last moments inertly,
Object of envy enormous
And of the tenderest pity,
Of love that was never yet equall'd
And of unquenchable hate.

Unstain'd by vile adulation,
Guiltless of cowardly outrage
Rises it, mov'd at the sudden
Disappearance of such a bright splendour,
And breathes at its urn what is destin'd
Perchance not to perish—a strain.

From the Alps to the Pyramid masses,
From fleet Manzanar to Rhine-water,
Of yon axe the terrible lightning
Was follow'd so dread by the thunder;
What a crash from Scilia to Tanais,
From one to the other main!

But was it true glory? O, leave to
Posterity such a hard question!
Let us bow, let us bow to the Maker,
Most Highest, who thought meet to imprint in
Him of his spirit creative
An image more vast and more plain.

The joy tempestuous yet trepid
Of a mighty design, the anxiety
Of a heart which boileth impetuously,
Whilst it thinks of the kingdom it finally
Wins, a prize thereby obtaining
Of which it were folly to dream.

All, all experienc'd he—glory
More great for the peril encounter'd,
Flight, the forerunner of victory,
The palace, presager of exile,
Twice in the dust you descry him,
Twice on the altar supreme.

As on the head of the shipwreck'd
Sailor the wild billow dashes,
The billow on which of the lost one
The lifted eye forward is straining,
Bent upon catching, though vainly,
A glimpse of the far-distant strand,

So is the accumulation
Of memories o'er that soul falling.
How often he unto posterity
Sought to narrate his proud actions,
And over the pages eternal
Sank weak and weary the hand.

O, how many times at the close of
A day by him spent in inaction,
His eyes with their lightning down lower'd,
His arms on his proud bosom folded,
He stood by remembrances haunted
Of days which had long ago been.

He thought and re-thought of the mobile
Pavilions, the ramparts in ruin,
The blaze of the bivouac faggot,
The neigh and the rush of the horses,
The rage of an empire insulted,
Soon eager to truckle, I ween.

Oh, perchance at such dreadful distraction,
All breathless had fallen the spirit
Despairing, but powerful from heaven
In pity a hand there descended,
A hand which the spirit transported
Into more breathable air,

And led it away by the flowery
Footpaths of hope to eternity's
Champains, unto the blest guerdon,
Of every desire the forestaller,
Where silence and darkness are flung o'er
Past glory's vain tumult and glare.

Lovely Faith, record thou this triumph
With liveliest joy, for though many
This triumph record with high pleasure,
Yet majesty surely so lofty,
To Golgotha's honour so hostile
Ne'er before humbled its knee.

O'er the inanimate ashes,
O man, no reproachful word utter;
The God who exalts and debases,
Who smiteth and then giveth comfort,
Upon the throne vacant beside him
Has plac'd him for ever, may be.

THE EYES OF SOPHY RIBEAUPIERRE

To kiss a pair of red lips small
  Full many a lover sighs;
If I kiss anything at all,
  Let it be Sophy's eyes.
The eyes, the eyes, whose witcheries
  Have filled my heart with care;
Too dear I prize the eyes, the eyes
  Of Sophy Ribeaupierre.

Were I the Czar, my kingly crown,
  My troops and victories,
And fair renown I 'd all lay down
  To kiss but Sophy's eyes.
The charming eyes, whose witcheries
  Have filled my heart with care;
Too dear I prize the charming eyes
  Of Sophy Ribeaupierre.

Perhaps I 've seen a fairer face,
  Though hers may well surprise;
A form perhaps of lovelier grace,
  But oh! the eyes, the eyes!
The matchless eyes, whose witcheries
  Have filled my heart with care;
I well may prize the matchless eyes
  Of Sophy Ribeaupierre.

What with the polished diamond-stone
  Can vie beneath the skies?

Oh, it is vied and far outshone
By Sophy's beaming eyes,
By Sophy's eyes, whose witcheries
Have filled my heart with care ;
Well may I prize the beaming eyes
Of Sophy Ribeaupierre.

The sun of June burns furiously,
And brooks and meadows dries ;
But, oh, with more intensity
Burn cruel Sophy's eyes !
The wicked eyes, whose witcheries
Have filled my heart with care ;
Too dear I prize the wicked eyes
Of Sophy Ribeaupierre.

O, soon beneath their piercing ray,
Like some parched plant which dies,
Wither shall I, poor youth, away ?
And all for Sophy's eyes.
But bless the eyes, whose witcheries
Have filled my heart with care ;
Till death I 'll prize and bless the eyes
Of Sophy Ribeaupierre.

EPIGRAM ON FOOLS

This world by fools is occupied,
And whom the sight of a fool displeases,
Within his chamber himself should hide,
And break his looking-glass to pieces.

TO DONA CLAMENZA

THE SONG ENTITLED THE SONG OF TRUTH

CLAMENZA Dame, to thee I 'll tell
The truths of what in the war befell—
  If so it please thy glorious beauty—
'Twixt Peter, King of High Leon,
Henry his brother of Aragon,
  And D'Ab Guesclin his comrade doughty.

And our brave boys, Moundinsa's boast,
Many of whom their good lives lost,
  To sing now what guerdon me entices ?
No flowers from thy fair hand I seek,
For them my merits are too weak,
  Thy friendship, Lady, me suffices.

In thirteen hundred and sixty-five
Charles-quint being King, who 's yet alive,
  March'd across our native region
The noble Lord Bertrand Guesclin
Baron of the Roc-Clarin
  With armed men a gallant legion.

Honor and faith and Jesu's love,
These were the motives them did move,
  To carry war o'er hill and valley
Against the cruel paynim crew ;
Those caus'd our brave Moundincans too
  Around their banner swift to rally.

God! those were stirring times and wild;
The women, who then were big with child,
  Wish'd they had forth their burdens given,
And that their babes in condition were,
The rattling quiver for them to bear
  And lances bright as stars of heaven.

Then left his parents many an heir,
Many left ploughs or fleecy care,
  Many left pursuits of learning,
Forsook his helpmate many a man,
From school then many a stripling ran,
  To wield the bow and arrow yearning.

The whole for our lov'd faith was done,
Therefore surprise there need be none
  The world display'd such store of mettle,
Since we have seen in olden tide
How for its sake more people died
  And more, yet more, of children little.

Full blythe of heart they all set out,
Thinking to have a pleasant bout,
  And gain old Spain the land of glory
Without a blow of sword or loss,
But you will hear that some grew cross,
  Ere ended, Lady, is my story.

Departed ere the sun was high
The Moundians all from San Sarny,
  The mass, the grand mass after hearing,
Zeal and devotion on each face,
Each bosom fill'd with God's dear grace,
  Right for Spain they departed, cheering.

In all they might be hundreds four,
'Mongst whom the men of greatest power
  And most esteem'd for feats I 'll wager,
Were bold Pagun, John Sarabel,
Simon Lautrec, Paul d'Auziell,
  Joan de Restra, Suan the Major.

They left the city soon behind,
Quarters in Ausetile they find,
  Thence speed they for Castelnau-darri ;
In Carcasone it is a hill,
Where Anjou's Duke with right good will
  Receiv'd them all and let them tarry.

A potent signor was the same,
Noble and brave of mighty fame,
  For the good King of France he lorded
In Languedoc, and he did aid
The armament which Guesclin led
  With everything the land afforded.

Then straight they wend for Perpignan,
Where they beheld upon the plain
  More than a thousand warriors merry,
Normans, Navarre-men and Gascons,
French Aragonians and Bretons,
  And at their head bold Spanish Harry.

With his brave comrades, such a band,
Each one of whom for two might stand,
  The King of Aragon was Harry,
Brother of fell Castilla's King,
Who basely from his couch did fling
  Blanche of Bourbon whom he did marry,

For lust of a fair Sarazine,
The daughter of King Bell-marine,
  And had the law of God discarded,
And to make Henry homage pay
For Aragon he did assay,
  Which fool-like he as his regarded.

Now in the land of Spain we are,
Where they are making dreadful war,
  But nought resists the arm of thunder,
The good cross-bow, the glittering lance
Of that nobility of France,
  Who fill the land with fear and wonder.

Guesclin crown'd Henry King of Spain,
But not without much blood and pain,
  And broke up all the Paynims banded,
But Peter 'scap'd and was not slow
To render him to fair Bordeaux,
  Where of his friends he help demanded.

The Prince of Wales has made a vow
That he for him would marvels do,
  And so he did, spurr'd on by fury
Against the French his foes who are ;
To Fontarbia through Navarre
  He pass'd along with whirlwind hurry.

He seiz'd King Peter of Navarre
And smote our gallants near and far,
  The battles gain'd his pride have flatter'd,
And finally to our bad luck
At Nadres such a blow he struck,
  That them he wholly broke and scatter'd.

Good Guesclin, Villanes, Deuchan,
He took with many a gentleman,
  And in his bosom reign'd no pity ;
Together fetter'd them he bore,
Amid a storm of insults sore,
  Unto Bordeaux his fenced city.

Henry escap'd and far from gay
Unto Provence has ta'en his way,
  The Pope he visits in Avignon.
From there he hied him up the Rhone,
The good Duke Bourbon in Narbonne
  Receiv'd him kindly 'neath his pinion.

Peter in pilgrim garb did go
To Guesclin prisoner in Bordeaux,
  And him address'd in guise most handsome,
Saying that he by right or wrong
With all his comrades brave or strong
  Would speedily be freed by ransome.

Said he to him the sum would bring
Though he should pawn his signet ring.
  Then Guesclin thanks and blessings giving,
Did loudly swear that briefly he
With all his comrades would be free,
  Or not be found amongst the living.

To seek the prince away he sped ;
The prince had risen from his bed
  And sat at meat in his pavilion ;
At ransome to be set he rav'd,
Said he would give whate'er was crav'd,
  Franks hundred thousand or a million.

For that to go from that bad place
He never hop'd by his good grace,
  Since he had him so foully treated,
Because in battle he o'erthrew
King Peter, the accursed Jew,
  Whom every one despis'd and hated.

The prince astonish'd at the words,
And yet more by the fierce regards
  Of Guesclin said, much anger showing,
'Just sixty thousand gold doubloons
I 'll have for thee and for thy loons.'
  Bold Guesclin then with fury glowing

Swore that to venge such treatment base
On Spaynish throne he 'd Henry place,
  Then hied around the coin to gather.
The King a hundred florins gave,
Yet more the Duke of Anjou brave,
  And something too the holy father.

He got from great, he got from small,
And ransom'd soon his comrades all,
  Then made as fast as he was able
For Spain ; bold Henry came there too,
With bands courageous, though but few,
  They set upon King Peter's rabble.

He with his country's native bands
And eighty thousand paynim hands
  Awaited them with scorn and laughter,
Confiding in his numerous powers,
Whom he thought better men than ours,
  Because of Nadres' deadly slaughter.

But the blinded wretch forgot that now
He lack'd the deadly English bow,
  For his former friends had from him retreated,
Because that when the day was gain'd,
To keep his word he had disdain'd
  And of their wages them had cheated.

But our brave men were not forlorne,
For all the miseries they had borne,
  Full confident through God's high favour
To smite their foemen and their king,
And from their sway the country wring,
  For God can do what He pleases ever.

And as they hop'd, so turn'd it out,
For in six months won Guesclin stout
  Burgos, Madrid, and all Castilla ;
Six battles won he with his blade,
Peter the King he prisoner made,
  Whose neck was sever'd at Sevilla.

Thus manifestly it appears
How wicked men do end their years,
  And how the mighty God rewards them.
They are accurst for evermore,
Whilst *he* for whom such love they bore
  Below no mercy shows towards them.

Whereas the men to God who pray
And who devotion's laws obey,
  When faintest is their expectation
Of good, behold it on them shower,
When they believe that all is o'er
  Then God from high doth send salvation.

Guesclin in prison who did groan,
Henrie abandon'd by his own,
The Lord reliev'd in strongest fashion ;
Guesclin deliver'd soon with store
Of vivers, money, men of power,
Crown'd Henry King of Spain's proud nation.

Congratulation Carloquint
Unto the brave De Guesclin sent,
And him appointed Marshal royal.
'I 've many a gallant cavalier,'
He said, 'but none who 's Guesclin's peer,
As has been prov'd by sharpest trial.'

Thus ended was in briefest space
The war with yonder miscrea[n]t race,
But not without a loss most scaring
Of cavaliers, our country's pride,
By thousands who in combats died,
Where they display'd their usual daring.

'Mongst whom most worthy of my strains
Are Matheu José-Lauvreins,
Who fighting died at bloody Nadres :
He was a valiant arbalest,
Who never slunk behind the rest,
But death has hurl'd him to his fathers.

Joan d'Ambres, a lance true bred,
Who at Burgos died the first, 'tis said,
Sieches, Monluc, Leon and Breffil,
Who at Madrid bid life good-bye,
Wept by their friends, I scarce know why,
To God they went, and not the Devil.

With Bernat Castelnau Marti,
Joan Carabodas Mondousi,
  Who 'midst the best had long been counted
For carrying far the lily flowers,
'Midst fields where arrows fell in showers,
  But who by death are now dismounted.

Two hundred of our Moundian train
Lie rotting on the roads of Spain,
  Besides full many a warrior noble
Of Normans, Navarre-men and Gascons,
French, Aragonians or Bretons,
  Whose loss fills many a land with trouble.

But I will now give o'er my strain ;
I see, fair Dame, I see full plain
  You grieve to hear the deaths so gory
Of such a number of brave men,
Whom now we need and shall agen,
  To guard of France the territory.

LOVE SONG

Yestere'en when the bat, and the owl, and his mate
Were holding discourse their small matters about;
And the sun, that the wee little stars might shine out,
Had extinguished the lamp of his lustre so great,

A shepherd exclaimed : 'O 'twas folly that I
My love should bestow upon one never kind,
Upon Liris the lovely, whose cold, cruel mind
Would suffer unmoved a true lover to die.

'Often times, when our flocks on the common did browse,
I 'd approach her to pour in her ear my fond vows,
But unto her companions to haste she was sure.
O, light of my eyes! wouldst thou render me blest,
And wouldst grant me two kisses on thy snowy breast,
I swear that each one should an hour endure!'

THE TRIUMPH OF THE MOUNDIAN

FAIR speech of Toulouse's fair city,
  More old than the tower of Nembro,[1]
God show to the monster no pity,
  Who thee on the dung heap would throw.
I am charm'd by thy high revelations ;
How great to thee my obligations !
I 'm in love with thee more every day,
And though Pegasus pleasure doth give me
'Tis only—let none disbelieve me,
When thou dost compose his array.

O language most cheering, endearing,
  Thy subtleties well thou dost know
Appeal to the soul through the hearing,
  For all must thy sweetness allow.
Of languages thou art the wonder,
All others to thee must knock under ;
Exert thy best powers and show
That wise were the people who nam'd thee
The Moundian, for so they proclaim'd thee
The tongue universal, I trow.

There are some that say Latin 's superior
  In every respect to Moundane—
I say that the Latin 's inferior
  And that with my blood I 'll maintain ;

[1] Nimrod.

To fanfaronade and to swagger
I scorn—but I carry a dagger
And I 'll prove in the face of the sun,
That the Tiber the half of its riches
At the sharing by Babylon's ditches
Had to yield to the nobler Garonne.

Moreover the soldier bald-headed,
   His name to the Cæsars who gave,
And who upon earth was more dreaded
   Than Mars the tremendous and brave,
By the sweetness was so captivated
Of the Moundian, as is related,
And by what he had learnt of its rules,
That those who the Moundian slighted
And in the coarse Latin delighted,
He treated as dunces and fools.

I know that the language in fashion
   In Paris, by some of our race
Is consider'd the language of passion,
   And the pink of all beauty and grace.
'Tis spruce, but it wanteth the phrases,
Alone to be found in these places,
Such allurements to dally and toy,
As of yore the great Jupiter sported
When Hebe forgetting, he courted
Young Ganny, the darling of Troy.

Some coxcombs are ceaselessly raising—
   God's blood, what a pestilent band !—
Their voices, and vilely dispraising
   The illustrious tongue of our land.

They say, 'midst one thing and another,
That of languages none she 's the mother,
Unlike one or two they adduce—
Well, she 's of no language the mother,
But of languages all the grandmother—
A clincher that for their abuse !

When Death, by whom quarter is given
  To none, our great Goudeli bard
Had transferr'd and transmitted to heaven,
  Homer, Virgil, and tuneful Rounsard.
The pas with our poet disputed,
But their foolish assurance he scouted,
Exclaiming in Moundian tongue :
' Pooh, pooh, what ridiculous pother !
Unto me, unto me and no other
The pas doth in justice belong.'

THE FRENCH PRINCESS

TOWARDS France a maiden went,
Towards France her course she bent,
Unto Paris,—there to find
Her father and her mother kind.

Far from any known abode
She had wandered from the road,
And rested on a blasted fir,
Waiting for some passenger.

Towards her came a cavalier,
He to Paris, too, did steer ;
When he met the maiden's eyes,
She address'd him in this guise :

' Wilt thou guide me, cavalier,
If to Paris thou dost steer ? '
' Will I guide thee, maiden fair ?
Yes, by all my hopes I swear.'

In the middle of the way,
He spoke to her of love and play ;
The maid, when she his suit had heard,
Cool'd him with a single word :

'Hush thee, hush thee, gentle knight!
Tho' I look so fair and bright,
Diseas'd I am,—diseas'd I came
From a tainted sire and dame.

'The mortal who with me shall lie
Will waste away until he die!'
The cavalier grew pale to see,
But not a sentence answer'd he.

The maid, when Paris was in sight,
Smil'd until she laughed outright.
'What makes thee smile?' the warrior said;
'What makes thee laugh, my pretty maid?'

'I laugh at the weak cavalier;
I hold in scorn the dastard's fear,
Who led me thro' the desert plains
And yet got nothing for his pains.'

The warrior's face with shame was dy'd;
He stammer'd and at length replied:
'We must return the way we 've crost,
For a something I have lost.'

'No,' answer'd she, 'I 'll not turn back,
To cross with thee yon desert track;
And even tho' we did return
Yet would treat thy love with scorn.

'Daughter of France's royal line,
I boast my birth from Constantine:
The man that makes me shed a tear
I reckon it will cost him dear.'

BERNARD'S ADDRESS TO HIS ARMY

FRESHLY blew the morning breeze,
When with all his Leonese,
Bernard went in war-array
To impede the Frenchman's way,

Who had come o'er hill and dale,
Urg'd by false Alfonso's tale,
To procure for him the throne,—
Just as if it were his own.

Not with yonder dastard train
But with Bernard rests our strain ;
Who, in accents deep and strong,
Thus address'd the assembled throng :

' Deck'd with buckler—bearing brand,—
Here like valiant men you stand,
For your country,—for your lives,—
For your king—and for your wives.

' If we fly, to-morrow's dawn
Sees our offspring led in scorn,
And with servile fetters bound,
By some haughty Gallic hound,

Who will strip, with forward glee,
All the bearings from our tree ;
And the lilies of his line
In their place will proudly shine.

' Shall the mountain, hill and wood,
Where our fathers' sires stood,
Now for lack of hearts and hands
Fall a prey to foreign bands ?

' He who with his single lance
Fears to meet three sons of France,
Let him turn ; with those that stay
Still I trust to win the day.

' I myself, this very hour,
Here engage to fight with four,
And to chase them o'er the plain
To their country back again.'

WAR-SONG

WRITTEN WHEN THE FRENCH FIRST INVADED SPAIN

Arise, ye sons of injur'd Spain,
And all your strength be summing,
For see ! along the distant plain
The foes of men are coming ;
Regardless of their haughty frown,
Rise, Biscay, rise ! and pour down
From every mountain's hoary crown
Your knights and caballeros.

'Tis said that in your veins the blood
Of Carthage pure is flowing ;
And will ye soil the noble flood
By Freedom's sweets foregoing ?
Fear not to meet yon Gallic host,
For England's sons, her pride and boast,
Will arm, and leave their native coast
To share your righteous battle.

Arise, arise ! the tyrants come
The peace of nations breaking ;
Tho' even now they feel at home
Their throne 's beneath them quaking.

Yes, yes ! their reign is nearly past,
Yet adder-like, unto the last
They seek the venom'd sting to cast,
And spread destruction round them.

What tho' above the bloody band
Religion's flag is streaming,
I guess their faith will never stand
Your faulchions' ruddy gleaming.
Then forward, forward, to the fight ;
And if you fall beneath their might,
'Tis sweet to die for home and right,—
For native land and freedom.

THE CID'S ENTRY INTO BURGOS

My Cid Ruy Dias entered the town of Burgos old ;
Behind him sixty pennants shone with silver and with gold.
To see the noble Campeador both men and women haste ;
Burgos dames and Burgos citizens were at the windows plac'd ;
But with no merry vivas, no shouts which rent the skies,
No show of snowy handkerchiefs except to wipe the eyes ;
All, all look'd very sorrowful, and cried with one accord :
'O God, what a good vassal, if he had but a good lord !'
To open door unto him no one the courage had,
For our monarch Don Alonzo was with my Cid stark mad.
A letter came to Burgos the very night before,
A fearful looking letter, the monarch's seal which bore,
Forbidding folks to show my Cid all hospitality,
Adding, whoever should him with the slightest thing supply,

Should have his goods ta'en from him, the eyes pluck'd from his face,
His body hung on gallows, his soul denied all peace.
Therefore no wonder Christian folks were fill'd with much dismay,
And 'stead of welcoming my Cid, to him did nothing say.

PEASANT SONGS OF SPAIN

I

WHEN Jesu our Redeemer
  To him the twelve did call,
By threes and fours he called them,
  Till they were mustered all.

And when they all were mustered,
  'Twas thus to them he spake :
' O which of ye, my children,
  Will perish for my sake ? '

Then, gazing on each other,
  They stood abashed and still ;
All save Saint John the Baptist,
  And Peter of the Hill.

' We 'll die for thee, O Jesus,
  Upon to-morrow's morn.'
For him died John the Baptist,
  And suffered pain and scorn.

II

THERE stands a stone, a rounded stone,
  'Midst ocean's surges hoary,
On which sweet Jesus set His foot
  When mounting to His glory.

There grows a rose, a blooming rose,
  'Midst ocean's briny waters,
That o'er may pass, to hear the mass,
  Havanah's dusky daughters.

THE SINGING MARINER

Who will ever have again,
On the land or on the main,
Such a chance as happen'd to
Count Arnaldos long ago?

With his falcon in his hand,
Forth he went along the strand;
There he saw a galley gay
Briskly bearing for the bay.

Ask me not her name and trade,—
All the sails of silk were made;
He who steer'd the ship along
Raised his voice, and sang a song.

Sang a song whose magic force
Calm'd the breaker in its course;
While the fishes, sore amazed,
Left their holes and upwards gazed.

And the fowl came flocking fast,
Round the summit of the mast;
Still he sang to wind and wave:
'God preserve my vessel brave!

' Guard her from the rocks that grow
'Mid the sullen deep below ;
From the gust, and from the breeze,
Sweeping through Gibtarek's seas.

' From the gulf of Venice too,
With its shoals and waters blue ;
Where the mermaid chants her hymn,
Borne upon the billow's brim.'

Forward stept Arnaldos bold,
Thus he spake, as I am told :
' Teach me, sailor, I entreat,
Yonder song that sounds so sweet.'

But the sailor shook his head,
Shook it thrice, and briefly said :
' Never will I teach the strain
But to him who ploughs the main.'

BELARDO'S WEDDING

FROM the banks, in morning's beam,
Of Xarama, famous stream ;
From the spot, or nigh it, where
It joins the Tagus broad and fair,
Sped Belardo, blithe and gay,
To receive the righteous pay
Of all the years of love he 'd spent
In doubts, and fears, and discontent—
But happy the shepherd who finally gains
The beautiful prize of his manifold pains.

Unto her village now he goes
The handsome Philis to espouse ;
For now her father, kind and bland,
But late so stern, yields him her hand.
Now in his eyes the shepherd shows
The rapture in his breast that glows,
That after storm and hurricane
The heaven should look bright again.
How happy the shepherd who finally gains
The beautiful prize of his manifold pains.

Not as of yore on foot, I trow,
Or in albarcas goes he now ;
Albarcas made of slain wolf hide,
In blood of cow or heifer dyed.

O snow-white pointed shoes wore he,
Green stockings gartered at the knee ;
Buttons composed of burning glass,
Presented, mind ye, by his lass.
How happy the shepherd who finally gains
The beautiful prize of his manifold pains.

What a knight of gallant air
Rides he forth on sorrel mare ;
Saddle of Friezeland leather made,
Fringe of the most dainty thread.
Sombrero new, of neatest shape,
Mantle long with lengthy cape,
Sayo green, obscure to see,
Graced with much embroidery.
How happy the shepherd who finally gains
The beautiful prize of his labour and pains.

By the guise in which he 's drest,
His hopes are visibly exprest ;
Hopes which so often damped and chilled
Are on the point to be fulfilled.
Within his bosom he doth bear
All the billets of his dear ;
They are so many bills which he
Is bent to settle speedily.
Happy the shepherd who finally gains
The beautiful prize of his manifold pains.

Arriving at the house he saw,
Waiting for him, his father-in-law,
Who, good-bye to scoffs and slights,
Holds his stirrup whilst he lights.

Lovely Philis at the door
Calls him ' husband ' and ' senor ';
He ' senora ' and ' dear wife '
Calleth her, they 're one for life.
Happy the shepherd who finally gains
The beautiful prize of his manifold pains.

THE MIRROR OF CINTRA

(*Translated from the original Portuguese on a marble slab in the garden of Don Juan de Castra, at Cintra.*)

TINY fields in charming order,
Which the jagged forests border ;
Sheltered valleys downward wending,
'Midst the rocks to heaven ascending ;
Silvery fountains turbid never,
Foliage dense which bloometh ever ;
Ceaseless Zephyrs gently playing,
Satyrs, fawns by thousands straying ;
Nymphs, with fair bewitching faces,
Form of Cintra's clime the graces.

1840.

THE VISION OF DON MANOEL

'Twould seem that He who dwells above the sun
To Manoel, as meed of merits rare,
Reserv'd this enterprise which urg'd him on
To movements vast and quick beyond compare.
Manoel, who of great departed John
The projects grand as well as crown did heir,
No sooner of the realm took charge than fain
He would essay the conquest of the main.

This monarch in his high and noble mind
The thought of the high duty ever bore,
Devolv'd by ancestry who still design'd
In all they did to add to Lusia's power,
No rest from its appealing e'er could find,
That thought held sway supreme and ne'er resign'd
Its place a moment even in the hour
Before the dawn, when stars which glitt'ring fall
To sleep invite the wearied mortals all.

'Twas then, just then, as Manoel lay on bed,
Where most distinct is ever fancy's train,
Still haunted by the thoughts, as I have said,
Of yonder obligation clear and plain,
His eyes by sleep were softly visited
Which did not fail to occupy his brain,
For whilst he slept by weariness o'erpower'd
Came there in various forms of dreams the Lord.

It seemed to him he mounted up so high
  That on the verge of the first sphere he stood,
Whence many worlds he saw before him lie
  And tribes of people numerous and rude,
And nigh to where the day has birth, full nigh,
  When he his eyeballs far had stretch'd, he view'd
From mountains ancient high their heads which rear
Two lofty founts arise of water clear.

Wild birds and beasts and steers of giant race
  Found habitation on the mountain side,
A thousand trees, of grass and shrubs, a maze,
  All intercourse and path to men denied ;
These lofty mountains show a hostile face
  To all approach and stand there in lonely pride,
Since Father Adam sinn'd before his God,
It might be seen they 'd not by man been trod.

Uprose, he thought, from those clear fountains cold,
  Moving, as if to him they would repair,
With lengthy strides two men exceeding old,
  Of rustic yet most venerable air ;
Great drops of water down their frames which roll'd
  Bathing them all cam[e] oozing from their hair ;
The colour of their skin was dusky brown,
Hirsute their beards, uncar'd for, overgrown.

Each on his brow a crown or chaplet bore,
  Of boughs and selcouth herbs we could not name ;
The one of them a wearied aspect bore,
  As one who from some distant region came,

So too his waters, which came on with roar,
  A birthplace far remote appear'd to claim,
E'en as Alpheus, though it joins the sea
In Syracuse, claims source in Arcadie.

This one, who did the noblest presence own,
  Address'd the King with voice that shook the air
From far : ' O thou to whose fair land and crown
  Is destin'd of the world a mighty share,
We two whose fame from East to West is blown,
  Whose necks were ne'er well humbled, yet declare
'Tis time for thee to send a gallant band
To claim and take fair tribute from our hand.

' The illustrious Ganges I, who in the clime
  Of heaven, O monarch, have my cradle true,
King Indus this, who in these hills sublime
  Is born, which here before thee thou dost view.
We 're doom'd to cost thee war, O King, and time,
  But pushing on at last thou shalt subdue
With manly heart and matchless victories
The various tribes which yonder meet thine eyes.'

The illustrious holy river said no more,
  Both in a moment disappear'd from sight ;
Manoel awakes with fear unknown before
  And perturbation of the heart not slight.
By this time Phoebus is extending o'er
  The sleeping hemisphere his mantle bright,
The King beholds with joy upon the sky
The morning parting flowers of ruddy dye.

The King to counsel calling all his Lords
  To them describ'd the forms in sleep he 'd seen,
And of the holy ancient (Ganges) tells the words,
  Which caus'd to all great wonderment, I ween.
But soon with loud acclaim and waving swords,
  It was resolv'd to launch a fleet with keen
Determin'd heroes mann'd, who o'er the foam
In quest of novel climes and hearths should roam.

THE EARTHQUAKE AT LISBON

What a spectacle was Lisbon, by a horrid earthquake tried,
Some idea of ancient Chaos she afforded at that tide:
A strange sound, a sound unusual, such as may be heard when hay
In savannahs scorch'd by summer falls to greedy fire a prey,
Or when waggon wheels are whirling, or when hosts the warfield tread,
Was the terrible announcer of the swift destruction dread,
Which did everything come over: with such fury did contend
The elements that frighten'd people screaming cried: 'The world 's at end!'
The firm earth is set in motion; how it trembles, how it quakes!
And of tremulous earth the motion the light air to tremble makes;
On the earth there is no standing—certain standing there is none,
Through the air no certain seeing, vague the object look'd upon.
See the ocean is engulfing yonder banks of lovely green,
Where of late prolific cattle calmly grazing might be seen:

Fire and flame are now exerting in sulphureous caves their might,
Old penascoes they are hurling down from many a giddy height :
The poor, honest, simple shepherd sees with wonder and despair
His dear meadows smoking, flaming, fluctuating here and there,
Whilst the cit[i]zen more polish'd feels his bosom fill'd with fear,
Lest another hill Vesuvius cloud with vapour Tagus clear.
Meanwhile proud imperial Lisbon, once of all the world the court,
Feels the horror of the onslaught, which to Satan was but sport,
Felt, that 's if perchance the sudden[n]ess of so dreadful, dire a blow
Would for such a thing as feeling any other time allow :
One moment, one, one single moment, but what can't a moment do ?
Swallows, closes up, down dashes, dashes down and shivers too
Here and there sweet hearths of comfort, towers which reach unto the sky,
Holy temples, stately pillars, proud palatial dwellings high :
The fall of broken walls, O horror ! by different ways doth thousands kill,
For though there be but one destruction, distinct each death-case still.

Some whilst quietly reposing in soft beds the
death-stroke feel,
Sleep here changing from death's image to that
dread thing death the real.
O how many wretches perish by their darling
household gods,
Things which once afforded shelter, now destroy
them—their abodes;
From the fall of some huge palace, O how
terrible the blow!
All the more disastrous making its huge size its
overthrow.
Many perish in the Temple, O just heaven, must
the floor
Of the Temple, pity's centre, like a butchery
stream with gore?
Would the wretched world were ended, since of
hope no gleam exists,
Gone are now the Temple's glories—altars, holo-
causts and priests.
Broken are the Doric columns, prostrate the
zimborios now,
Fallen the roofs, which in their falling shatter'd
everything below.
Ah, in Lisbon there 's no refuge, grim death
triumphs, well may he,
Since the monster's foot has enter'd the thrice
blessed sanctuary;
In the streets how many hundreds from the world
departure take,
Some whilst running, some whilst walking, some
as they were looking back;

Many perish'd hid in cellars, many perish'd on the quays ;
To be brief, full many perish'd where death happen'd them to seize.
Everywhere speeds consternation, tracing on the human face
Surprise, astonishment, confusion, haggard fear and wild amaze :
See how yonder man is struggling with great arms robust to free
From a heap of stones his body, struggling unsuccessfully ;
One is stumbling, one is falling, in the air another swings,
Dangling from a plank he 's hold of ; frantic'ly a woman flings
From on high herself down headlong ; whilst another to her love,
To her consort calls for succour, and a third to God above,
Whilst a fourth dies, hapless creature, not from outward injury,
Not from blow of beam or rafter, but from mental agony.
Undecided stands the miser 'twixt the love of life and pelf ;
Fain he 'd carry off his riches, gladly he would save himself ;
If he tries to save his riches, he cannot from danger run,
So he standeth doing neither, till the time for action 's gone.

Avaricious Jason yonder doth his caitiff shoulders
load
With accursed golden metal, there he trudges
bending, bow'd,
There he trudges gasping, panting, till at length
he fainting falls,
Buried 'neath a load of riches, and a mass of
broken walls.
The observer good and pious of the Law by
heaven approv'd,
By two influences most urgent, but most different,
touch'd and mov'd,
In the care of the bless'd images and of valued
life employs
All the energies left in him in that hour of dread
surprise ;
Carefully the immortal cargo takes he in his pious
hands,
And undaunted through a tempest shower of
stones and flaming brands,
Yet more happy than Eneas to a place of refuge
brings
His own life and what he values far, far more, the
sacred things.
The fastidious damsel yonder, who ne'er ventures
in the street,
Save she sallies forth bedizened, or as she would
term it neat,
Three times to the portal goeth, three times
turneth in distress,
That she may pick up to deck her some neglected
piece of dress,

Going, stopping and lamenting 'twixt contending feelings two,
Vanity and fear, behold her, undetermined what to do,
Neither staying nor departing, still irresolute there is she,
Till she parts with dear life rather than with dear propriety.
More than ever touch'd with pity, of all gentle feelings best,
The chaste matron warmly presses her dear infant to her breast;
Hoping that the little trembler, 'midst the elemental strife,
May extract some drop of comfort to prolong its feeble life;
But see Nature's Law perverted, swooning on the rugged stone,
She the granite hard embraces 'stead of her beloved son,
Whilst the son, the little trembler, from her wounded breast instead
Of the kindly milk maternal sucks the bitter life-stream red.
Shouts the father, shouts the master, loftily and proudly calls
The prime minister, the captain bellows till he 's hoarse and bawls,
But nor son nor servant answers, nor official slave replies,
And the soldier not a stiver cares for his commander's cries.

All, all is disorder, horror; and now comes a
 curse as dire
Almost as the cruel earthquake, hither comes
 consuming fire,
To devour with savage fury what of Lisbon now
 remains—
Broken hearts and broken houses, broken palaces
 and fanes.
Furiously it catches hold of all it meeteth in its
 path,
And to ashes all reduces, nothing can resist its
 wrath.
See it preys on things most precious, things far
 India's coasts provide,
Things which in a thousand vessels Ganges sends
 to Tagus wide.
O the dreadful conflagration, O the smoke that
 seem'd from hell,
But why longer on horrors of that day of terror
 dwell?
I now hasten to inform you, mortals to confess
 were driven
That for help in such a trouble man must only
 look to heaven.
Mov'd by yonder truth eternal starts the stupid,
 kneels the wise,
One shows sense, the other reverence for the Ruler
 of the skies;
He, whom thunder's voice nor lightning's glitter
 scarcely could awake,
Finds his hearing, now he 's stricken by the earth's
 tremendous quake;

He, who into Nature's mysteries was most eager
to enquire,
Seeks yon portent's cause in God and leaves the
subterranean fire.
The same thing all, all are doing, although they
oppos'd may be,
Through their false creeds, to each other, creeds
of strange variety;
For the God who sits in heaven, when He designs
of His great might
To display a ray, a sample, all religions can
unite:
The dark Jew, the Hebrew vagrant who still
calculates the weeks
Mystical of which great Daniel in his scroll
Chaldaic speaks,
Little thinking, whilst he 's pond'ring best their
period to extend,
With how little, little profit he the fleeting time
doth spend,
The Agarene, O the perfidious, O the vile and
hateful Moor,
Who of Christ is ever willing to confess the
sovereign power,
And who unto Him concedeth th' attributes of the
Most High—
Mark the impudence — invested in simple
humanity,
The rich Englishman and all the nations of the
chilly North,
Nations justly fam'd for science and for sterling
deeds of worth,

But who rather from false honour than from reason's force renew
The delirious dreams of Arius, chief of the schismatic crew—
In a word all, all the nations which the world to Lisbon sends
To extract the gold it loves so, and when gotten so mis[s]pends,
Raise in various tongues their voices, and in frantic wild alarm
Recognise in full the power of the dread Almighty arm.
In this one point there 's agreement, in this one point one accord,
Though in every other matter, they 're at dagger and at sword ;
Woe, woe, woe that man has need of frequent visitations stern :
Woe, woe, woe that him to awaken earth must quake and Lisbon burn ;
Lisbon, thou who whilom wast of Lusitania's sons the home,
Who didst oft afford asylum to the bravest hearts of Rome,
Whilom of the Moor the fortress, then the court where monarchs great,
Fenc'd around by thousand heroes, liv'd in truly regal state,
Thou to all the world who, giving laws, high laws, a Queen didst reign,
Who didst send across the billows of the unfathomable main

Shrines of blessed saints and martyrs in tall ships
with gilded prows,
Unto regions yet more distant than where fleet
Hydaspes flows—
Lisbon 's lost. Ah, hapless Lyzia! Who now
lives for thee to care?
Did Death kindly take thy children, rivers of salt
tears to spare?
Well perhaps amid thy ruins to entomb these
scenes of woe,
That all feeling may be smother'd by thy very
overthrow.
But thy fall, O hapless city, was, alas! of such a
kind
That it never, never, never can be blotted from
the mind.

THE INFERNO

CANTO V

From the first circle I departed now
  Into the second, which is not so great
And where there 's howling less, though far more
    woe.

Gnashing his teeth stands Minos at the gate ;
  He cringes, examines, judges and commands
In strict accordance with the offence's weight.

Here I must say that when before him stands
  The lost soul, it must all its guilt avow,
And he who all crime fully understands,

Knowing whereto in Hell it ought to go,
  Girds him as many times with his curl'd tail
As the degrees he 'd have it stow'd below.

Always before him stand poor ghosties pale,
  Who each in turn confess, their venture hear,
Then, snatch'd away, are tumbled down to wail.

'O thou who com'st to misery's dark mansion
    drear,'
  Said Minos, as on me he cast his glare,
Desisting from his duty, high, severe,

'Mind how thou com'st and whom thou trust'st beware,
Let not the entrance wide delude thine eye.'
'No more,' exclaim'd my guide with lofty air,

'To stay his fated walk let no one try;
It is decreed above where everything is decreed,
That 's will'd, is possible. So no reply.'

Now are we brought by our strange journeying
Where first the cries of woe the ears affright;
We 're entering the place from whence they spring.

A place it was devoid of every light,
Which bellow'd as doth bellow the salt deep,
When it is beat by furious winds that fight.

The hellish tempest, which ne'er doth sleep,
Drives on before it crowds of spectres poor,
Tumbling them over pell mell, heap on heap.

But when they came that ruin'd pile before,
O then what wailing shouts and shrieks arise,
What curses on the holiest name they shower.

This kind of torment was for those, I trow,
Who, unto carnal practices inclin'd,
Unto their lusts and not their reason bow,

And as some flock of birds by wintry wind
Are hurried up and down and to and fro,
E'en so these hapless ghosts of evil kind

Are bustled here and there and high and low,
  No ray of hope e'er cheers their wretched mind,
Not of repose, but even lesser woe.

And, as the cranes when the sun has declin'd,
  Fly o'er the moors and sing their plaintive song,
E'en so those wretched ghosts no rest that find

Approach us now, a wild and wailing throng.
  'Who are those people,' said I to my guide,
'By the wind's fury slung about and flung?'

'The first of them you ask about,' replied
  My guide, 'was the imperial lady high
For speaking languages fam'd far and wide.

'So given was she to all unchastity,
  That legal by a law the vice she made,
To do away with her own infamy.

'The wife was she of Ninus, as we read,
  And his successor o'er the lands she rul'd,
Which by the Turkish Soldan now are sway'd.

'The next was she who kill'd herself, befool'd
  By love, untrue to poor Sicheus' shade,
Cleopatra in the ways of lust well school'd.'

I Helen saw, the cause of ruin dread,
  And I the mighty Achilles spied,
Ever by love so sorely buffeted.

I Paris saw and Tristan, and my guide
  Did point to and did name a thousand more,
Who for the sake of carnal love had died.

Now when the dames and cavaliers of yore
I had been shown, I heav'd a doleful sigh,
So keenly pity touch'd my bosom's core.

At length I said : ' Sir Poet, fain would I
Discourse with yon two, who together come
And seem in swiftness with the wind to vie.'

Then he to me : ' When nearer through the gloom
They draw, enquire of them and thou wilt know
What kind of love has brought them to their doom.'

Soon as the wind towards us them did blow,
I rais'd my voice and cried : ' Ye souls distrest,
Come and speak to us, unless fate say no.'

As doves come flying to their much lov'd nest,
Call'd by their young ones' cries, with wings outspread,
Urg'd by affection and by ardent zest,

So from the band in which poor Dido pin'd
Those twain came flying through the scowling sky,
So strongly work'd on them the summons kind.

' O thou of gentlest heart and mildest eye
Who visitest amidst these scenes of care
Us whom the world us'd, O so cruelly,

' For thy soul's rest to heaven's king a prayer
We 'd breathe, if he were not our enemy,
Since thou hast pity on a wretched pair.

'Say what thou wish'st, attention I will ply,
  You 'll speak to us and we will answer you,
Now the wind 's hush'd, which lately blew so high.

'The land is plac'd, where first my breath I drew,
  Nigh to the shore where down the broad Po hies,
Repose to seek, with all its streamlet crew.

'Love, who makes soon the gentle heart his prize,
  Inspir'd this youth with love of the form fair,
Soon taken from me and in horrid guise.

'Love, who the one that 's lov'd doth seldom spare,
  Inspir'd my heart with love for him so great
That as you see he 's with me everywhere.

'Love 'twas brought us to the self-same fate!
  O Cain attend who our destruction wrought.'
Such were their words, the poor disconsolate.

Now when these troubled souls to end had brought
  Their tale, I droop'd my head and held it low,
Until the poet said: 'What 's in thy thought?'

At length I cried, 'Alas, I wonder how
  Many sweet thoughts and fond desires led
Them to the step which caus'd their present woe.'

Then turning unto them my face, I said:
  'Francesca, these thy frightful miseries
Make me soft pity's saddest tears to shed.

'But tell me, in the hour of balmy sighs
  To what did love, the crafty god, impel,
And by what mean conduct that ye did know

'Your dubious wishes.' 'Grief more fell
There 's not than to recall in time of woe
One's happy days, and that your guide knows well.

'But as our love so strong a wish ye show
To be acquainted with from its first root,
Like one who speaks and weeps I 'll even do.

'One day we read how knightly Lancelot
On cruel Love's account much torment bore.
We were alone and suspected not.

'More than one time reading caus'd us our
Eyes to lift up and chang'd our colour, one,
And only one, it us did overpower.

'When we did read the smile the cheek doth don,
When one is kiss'd by him we do adore,
He, whose dear shade waits ever mine upon,

'Did kiss my lips, though trembling all o'er.
"Curs'd be the book and curs'd its scribe," cry I,
After that day we read it never more.'

Whilst this poor soul breath'd thus its history,
The other sprite so grievously did moan
That I for pity felt as I should die,
And fell, as bodies fall, when life is flown.

SONNETS

I

When Alexander reach'd the funeral mound
  Of great Achilles, with a sigh he cried :
'Blessed he sleeps, for he a poet found,
  Worthy to waft his glory far and wide !'

But this same dove with purest beauty crown'd,
  Whose equal ne'er upon earth's breast was spied,
From my poor lyre must hear her praises sound—
  How seldom justice human lot doth guide !

Her, whom high Homer or sweet Orpheus bard,
Or he the shepherd Mantua joys to claim,
Might count it honour through all time to sing,

An ugly star, an adverse fate and hard,
Consigns to one who worshippeth her name,
But sullies it each time he wakes the string.

II

Say from what mine drew love the yellow gold
To form those tresses ? From what thorn bush tore
Those roses sleek ? And from what Alp-peak hoar
Those stainless snows which seem no longer cold ?

From whence the pearls, which serve to break and hold
Sweet words and strange, like those of other shore ?
From whence the beauties, O how great their store,
On that calm forehead not of mortal mould ?

And from what angels and what sphere that lay
Of heaven, whose sweetness doth this frame destroy,
So that but little now remains to me ?

From what sun burst the kind but haughty ray
Of those bright eyes, from whence my grief and joy,
Which freeze and burn my heart alternately ?

LINES

'Repent, O repent!' said a Friar one day
To a reprobate wretch, as expiring he lay;

'As I came up the stairs, I was frightened to see
The devil who 's waiting to seize upon thee.'

'You saw him then truly?' 'Too truly, alas!'
'And under what shape?' 'Under that of an
ass.'

'Well, well!' cried the sinner, 'I am not afraid,
You 've only been terrified by your own shade.'

RINALDO TAKES TO THE HIGHWAY

One day as with Rinaldo Oliver
  Did play at chess, as sometimes was his use,
Differ'd about a move the knightly pair,
  And straight a scene of hot dispute ensues.
At last Sir Oliver to Amon's heir
  Said : 'You are as scant of brains as any goose,
And always to defend the wrong, employ
Bluster and noise—I 'm not your stable boy !'

Rinaldo answer'd : 'Doubtless you suppose,
  Because Meridiana nigh doth stand,
You run no risk ?' Then wild the quarrel grows,
  And pretty words of villany they band
Until Sir Oliver to t' other's nose
  Advanc'd his fist ; the damsel seiz'd his hand—
Up sprang Rinaldo with a furious roar,
Sir Oliver straight bolted through the door.

To seek his armour he is only gone,
  He soon return'd and forth his brand he drew ;
It chanc'd Rinaldo at his belt had none,
  Meanwhile Orlando rush'd between the two.
Meridiana trembled and took on.
  Soon Charles arriv'd and at Rinaldo flew.
'Each day thou dost disturb my court,' he said,
'Art ever wrong, and load'st with shame my head!'

Rinaldo who had well nigh lost his mind
  With [rage] replied to Charlemagne, 'You lie!
'Tis he is wrong; to slay me he design'd.'
  Then shouted to his people Charles the high,
'Unless this felon hound ye take and bind,
  I'll give ye precious cause to weep and cry!'
Rinaldo said, 'If any one come near,
A precious box I'll give him on his ear!'

Orlando saw his cousin sore in need
  And spoke him thus—'Unless thou wouldst be caught,
I pray thee to Montalban straight to speed,
  Charles, I perceive, is with such fury fraught,
That who is wrong or right he does not heed.'
  Rinaldo, wasting little time in thought,
Bayardo took, Orlando's word obey'd,
And at full gallop for Montalban made.

Charles at Orlando show'd displeasure great,
  For having caus'd the culprit thus to fly,
'Why didst not leave the traitor to his fate?'
  Said he, 'He'll now each day my beard defy!
Thee as a fool I from this day shall rate.'
  Then summoning his council hastily,
In a brief speech he ask'd what should be done,
In this emergency, with Amon's son.

Orlando said, 'Now be advis'd by me,
  Leave him but time his arrogance to rue,
And you shall quickly have him on his knee,
  And for his pardon hear him humbly sue.'

King Charles replied, ' Should I to this agree,
He 'd quickly give to me this lie anew ;
I in my court will harbour him no more,
But will pursue him till I shed his gore.'

Namo at last gave it as his advice,
He should be banish'd from the courtly sphere,
For fear some other danger should arise,
Or evil happen yet more sad and drear.
Said he : ' A rumour 'mongst the people flies,
Another pagan swarm would straight appear,
And he might breed some tumult in that case,
Since he 's the darling of the populace.'

Astolfo would not him an outlaw make,
But wish'd the King should pardon him in all,
Whilst Oliver 'gainst Astolfo spake,
In such a guise as highly rais'd his gall.
Charles order'd they should Namo's counsel take,
And outlaw him before they left the hall.
One single word escap'd from Gano's tongue,
' The lie he gave to you,—so have him hung ! '

Soon as Astolfo saw his words were vain
And that against Rinaldo Charles was fell,
He would no longer idly there remain,
And hurried to Montalban him to tell
How to besiege him they had counsel ta'en,
And from the country afterwards expel ;
Moreover, what infernal counsel gave
To Charlemagne, Sir Gan the traitor knave.

A thousand times to God Rinaldo swore
  That he some time would vengeance wreak condign
On that same wretch with every crime stain'd o'er,
  If God should further life to him assign.
That said, 'Sweet Cousin, as none loves me more
  Than thou, I 'll tell thee of a plan of mine,—
It is that we should rob the country round,
And lead a life like robbers most renown'd.

'And if Saint Peter in our path we see
  We 'll strip him bare and crack his crown beside,
Bold Riccardetto of our troop will be.'
  'Why waste the time in prate?' Astolfo cried,
'I 'll rob Ottoni for a marvadi.
  To-morrow we to rob will take a ride,
We 'll neither comrade nor relation spare,
And afterwards the booty we will share.

'And if Saint Ursula with her train should pass
  Along with Angel Gabriel, who of old
Said to the Virgin Mary "Hail! Sweet lass!"
  We 'd spoil the ladies and to take make bold
His cloak!' Rinaldo said, 'By Balaam's ass,
  In thee a godsend, brother, I behold;
I see thou 'rt wise and that thy mettle 's good,
  Sure thou hast oft already prowl'd the wood?'

Malgigi, who was there, put in his word,
  And said, 'No plan could be devis'd more sound.'
Rinaldo 'listed people of the sword,
  Soon all the outlaws gather'd him around;

Gentry, each one of whom deserv'd the cord,
  Within Montalban sure asylum found.
He gave them clothes and best of drink and meat,
So that his band was in a month complete.

For fear of him the people scarce could sleep,
  Each day was heard of some disaster sad,
This one was slain and robb'd in forest deep,
  This other lost his ears and all he had,
Byzants, five score, in sight of Paris keep.
  I need not say that traitor Gan was glad;
He hop'd that Charles yet more enrag'd would
    grow,
And to besiege him in Montalban go.

IN PRAISE OF WARLIKE VIRTUE

I WOULD not reverence nor would praise a man
 For wrestling-prowess and for speed of pace,
Though huge and mighty as the cyclop clan,
 Or could he distance Boreas,

Not if more lovely he than Tithon were,
 More rich than Midas, as Cinyras wise,
More kingdoms had than Pelops 'neath his care,
 Spoke in Adrastus's own honeyed guise,

Not if each gift he had save courage high,
 For none can be illustrious in war,
If seeing death he dare not bravely die
 And 'gainst the foemen stretch his weapons far.

Valour best virtue is to mortal stem
 And most becoming a young man indeed ;
He is a city's brightest, proudest gem
 Who to the foremost ranks of war shall speed,

And there remaining scorn to basely fly,
 Trusting in courage and audacious mind,
Who falling cheers his comrade, standing by :
 Thus shall a man in battle glory find.

Quickly he puts the hostile bands to flight,
  The billows of the war he scatters round ;
He dies, amidst the hottest of the fight,
  Blessing his parents and his native ground,

Pierced through his breast and through his moony shield,
  And his cuirass with many a gory wound,
To him both young and old their tears shall yield
  And all the city shall in grief be found.

All shall revere his children and his tomb,
  His children's children and their progeny,
Nor o'er his fame shall sweep oblivion's doom,
  Though under earth he shall immortal be,

Who 'neath the hand of Mars resign'd his breath,
  More bold and brave than other mortals seem ;
But if he chance to 'scape somniferous death,
  The brightest meed is his that men can dream.

To yield him honour every youth essays,
  To Hades sinks he, tasting much that 's sweet ;
He rules the cities in his latter days
  And none would rob him of the reverence meet.

Young men and others more advanc'd in age,
  When in their seats, arise to give him place.
Let him not fear the dreadful war to wage,
  Who fain would be the foremost of his race.

HARMODIUS AND ARISTOGITON

WITH the leaves of the myrtle I 'll cover my brand,
Like Harmodius and Aristogiton of yore;
When the tyrant they slew, and their dear native land
They caused with just laws to be govern'd once more.

O, beloved Harmodius! thou still art not dead;
In the Isles of the Blest thou still livest, they say,
Where the swift-heel'd Achilles and bold Diomed
Through sweet flowery meadows continually stray.

With the leaves of the myrtle I 'll cover my blade,
Like Harmodius and Aristogiton of yore;
Who, whilst the high rites to Athena were paid,
The bold tyrant Hipparchus extended in gore.

And on earth ever, ever your glory shall glow,
Harmodius and Aristogiton, sun-bright;
Because ye the damnable tyrant laid low,
And restored to your country her law and her right.

ODE

THE earth to drink does not disdain,
The trees drink of the earth full fain.
Of the light air the sea drinks free,
The red sun drinketh from the sea,
And the red sun, at pride of noon,
I 've seen drunk up by the pale moon.
Then why, friend, with me prove in ire,
That I to drink, too, feel desire.

THE DEATH OF ADONIS

Fell Cithera to crying,
  Adonis when she view'd
With pallid features lying,
  With tresses blood-embrued.
Her grief on madness borders,
  But 'midst her trouble sore
The attendant loves she orders
  To bring to her the boar.

Through all the forest tangled
  With winged speed they hied ;
The beast the boy who mangled
  They quickly found and tied.
How prettily they 're mauling
  The hapless monster now ;
This one his neck is hauling,
  This beating him with bow.
The Queen of beauty mighty
  Unwilling drew he nigh.
To him said Aphrodita,
  With vengeance in her eye :

' Thou savagest of creatures
  In all the forest's bound,
Behold those lifeless features !
  Behold that gory wound !
Tell me, thou sylvan rover,
  Before I bid thee die,
Why didst thou kill my lover ?
  Why didst thou wound his thigh ? '

The beast with gesture humble,
  For much he stood in fear,
Did forth this answer mumble :
  ‘ O, Cithera, I swear
By yonder form of beauty,
  Which lieth lifeless there,
These loves who pay thee duty,
  These fetters which I bear,
I never dreamt of harming
  Thy lov'd and handsome youth ;
A graven image charming
  I deem'd his form, forsooth.

A heat it did engender,
  I 'd kiss the naked thigh,
I thought to kiss it tender,
  But gor'd it terribly.
The tusks to thee I proffer,
  Which work'd thy darling woe ;
Why teeth about me suffer,
  Which dare with love to glow ?
Wouldst further expiation,
  Cut off these lips of mine ? ’
Then sweet commiseration
  Felt Cithera divine.

She made the loves release him
  And words of kindness said.
Her kindness well did please him,
  With her he ever staid.
He left the woods and bushes
  And follow'd in her train,
And burnt his amorous tushes
  Within her sacred fane.

IN PRAISE OF ROME

HAIL, Mars's daughter! hail, O Rome!
Bedeck'd with diamond crown,
Who sitt'st enthron'd, a splendid Queen,
On height Olympian, ne'er I ween
Thence to be tumbled down.

To thee alone old Fate from first
Did grant the glorious meed
Of sway, which nought should break or bow,
That fill'd with might and vigour Thou
Of all might'st take the lead.

Hail, hail! with chains of potency
The broad backs thou dost bind
Of earth and of the ocean tide.
Thou dost with ease and safety guide
The cities of mankind.

Time, mighty time, which all o'erthrows,
Which doth the pristine lot
Of all things change, as it may please,
O mighty Rome, the prosperous breeze
Of fortune alters not.

For thou alone of all, of all
Enceint by mighty, mighty men,
Dost great and mighty men forthbring,
Who armed with spears from thy womb spring,
Like bristling crops of grain.

THE PUNISHMENT OF CUPID

(*A Fragment*)

AND Sappho from Leucate's stormy steep,
Burning with love for Phaon, threats to leap.
Bastard Harmonia's ornamental gear [1]
Sad Eriphyle doth refuse to wear,
She her son's bane nor yet her husband's weal.
Of airy Crete the whole Minoian tale [2]
Vibrates in picture-guise before the view :
Pasiphae must the snow-white bull pursue.
The thread deserted Ariadne bears,
Roll'd up within her hand, whilst Phaedra stares
Wildly upon the tablet-leaves thrown down ;
This bears a halter, this a shadowy crown,
The tinge of shame o'erspreads the other's brow
That once she enter'd the Dedalian cow.

[1] The necklace of Harmonia, daughter by adultery of Mars and Venus, was endowed with a fatal property, for whosoever possessed it shortly came to a miserable end. For the sake of this necklace Eriphyle betrayed the lurking-place of her husband, the prophet Amphiaraus, whither he had retired in order to avoid being compelled to the Theban war, foreseeing that he should perish if he went. Upon his departure he commanded his son Alchmeon to take vengeance upon his mother as soon as he should receive intelligence of his death, which command the son fulfilled.

[2] The story relating to Minos, King of Crete, viz. the adventure of his wife Pasiphae and his two daughters Ariadne and Phaedra, which being generally known does not require to be detailed.

Laodamia, regal fair, two nights,
Soon past in unsubstantial delights,
Of a deceas'd and living husband craves.[1]
In other spot, all fierce with naked glaives,
Thisbe [2] and Canace [3] affright and she
Eloza [4] sprung from Sidon of the sea ;
This bears a husband's, this a father's brand,
And this a guest's escap'd from Trojan strand.
And there roams, as she once on Latmia's mount
To influence Endymion's sleep was wont,
Luna [5] with torch and star-set diadem.
A hundred others congregate with them,
Who opening wounds of ancient loves again,
Cherish with sweet and mournful plaints their pain.
'Midst of whom suddenly rash Cupid stray'd,
With clanging wings dispelling the thick shade.
They know the boy, and memory tells them all,
That he 's to them a common criminal.
Although the hurried clouds around that swim
The girdle sparkling with gold knobs bedim,
The quiver too and eke the torches glow :
They know him yet : and straight begin to show

[1] Protesilaus, the first of the Grecians slain in the Trojan war. Laodamia his wife entreated of the Gods that he might be revived for the space of one day, in order that she might discourse with him, which request was granted.

[2] See Ovid's *Metam.*, lib. iv.

[3] Daughter of Eolus, king of the wind. She killed herself with her father's sword, which he had sent to her upon discovering her incestuous intercourse with her brother.

[4] Dido, who stabbed herself with the sword of Æneas.

[5] Luna bicornis, who it is said lulled to sleep the youth Endymion upon Mount Latmos, that she might caress him whilst sleeping.

A spectral strength : and hastening to form
Phalanxes dense, upon their foe they storm,
A foe caught far from heaven's blissful home,
Errant and lost amid the vaporous gloom,
And him excuses vainly proffering
Into their centre's custody they bring
The highest myrtle in that sad grove found,
One for the punishments of Gods renown'd,
They choose. Prosperine crucified of yore
Adonis there for loving Venus more.
Suspended to its trunk the lovely child,
His hands tied 'hind his back and screaming wild,
With ropes drawn taut his tender feet around,
They ply with punishment which knows no bound.
Love by no judge accus'd, and innocent
Is guilty—each to clear herself is bent,
And to another's fault her own crime lays.
All, all with imprecations haste to raise
The tokens of their death, revenge they call
To punish the disease which prov'd their fall.
This bears a nooze, an airy faulchion this
Thrusts forth, or crag which visionary is,
Or empty sea or water-lacking lake.
These prefer flames, and 'gainst the trembler shake
Torches with no fire hissing, till his breast
The myrrh-tree open'd all with tears opprest,
And o'er the body of the suffering one
The amber of the weeping trunk is thrown.
Some in comparison forgiving, seek
Merely for sport, that 'neath a needle's prick

. . . . .

THE FISH

FROM the palace that 's under the trees
  See the maiden distracted race,
Her hair flutters wild on the breeze,
  And streaming with tears is her face.

The end of the forest she gains,
  Where the rivulet falls in the lake,
She wrings her white hands and complains,
  With a heart that is ready to break.

' O down in thy watery bower,
  Fair Switezanka, the maid,
List, list, in this terrible hour
  To the voice of a damsel betray'd.

' I lov'd my lord dearer than life,
  And ever to love me he swore,
But he taketh a princess for wife
  And Krysia drives from his door.

' Let him joy in his youthful career
  And toy with his beautiful dame,
But ah ! let him never come here,
  To sport with my anguish and shame.

'What hope in the world can there be
  For the minion discarded wild,
Fair Switezanka, to thee
  I haste—but my child—ah! my child.'

O then she did bitterly weep,
  And her hands placing over her eyes
She plung'd her at once in the deep,
  Which drown'd in a moment her sighs.

From the woods where the palace doth stand
  A thousand lamps brilliantly glance,
There meets a convivial band
  With music, with shout and with dance.

But amidst the loud glee of the rout
  Shouts the cry of a child on the ears;
From the wood a grey servant comes in,
  In his arm a fair infant he bears.

To the water directs he his way,
  Where the willows entwining so close
The sides of the river array,
  In its serpent-like course as it flows.

There he stands in the dark shady nook
  And exclaims with a face of despair:
'Ah! who to the babe will give suck?
  Where art thou, O Krysia, where?'

'I am here in the depths of the flood,'
  A voice sweet and gentle replied;
'Where the cold is congealing my blood,
  And greedy worms gnaw out my eyes.

' 'Midst pointed stones, wormlets and eels
  The wild billows carry me on,
Flies and corals must serve for my meals,
  My drink is the cool dew alone.'

But still as he stands in the nook
  The grey servant exclaims in despair :
' Ah ! who to the babe will give suck,
  Where art thou, O Krysia, where ? '

But what is that rushing so bright
  Through the transparent womb of the deep,
The water is troubled and bright,
  A fish is seen upward to leap.

Like a flint which I 've seen a boy fling,
  A boy that was nimble of wrist,
Our fish with a bound, with a spring,
  The wet surface gracefully kiss'd.

The body with gold bedropt all
  Showeth fins of the ruddiest dye,
The head as a thimble is small,
  As a grain is each glittering eye.

But she puts off the scaly fish coat,
  Again is a fair demoiselle,
From her dear head the light tresses flow,
  How her bosom and dainty neck swell !

On her cheeks beauty's roses you see,
  Her breasts milk-white apples they seem,
'Neath the middle a mere fish is she,
  'Neath the branches she swims in the stream.

Her hands the poor baby receive,
Which she hastes 'neath her bosom to place :
'Lullaby, little dear, do not grieve,
Lullaby, O thou dear little face.'

When silent the baby became,
She hangs on a bough stretching o'er
The basket, makes tiny her frame
And her fair head compresses once more.

Again she has dight her in scales,
And feelers appear at each side,
She dives, and a few water bells
Only rise on the face of the tide.

Thus ever at eve and at morn,
When the grey servant stands in the nook,
Does Switezanka return
To her babe, to her babe to give suck.

But one sweet sunny evening, O why
Comes he not, as he 's wont, on the green ?
The usual time 's come and gone by,
Yet he with the child is not seen.

To the spot he can't come and must wait,
Impatient and little content,
The Lord and the Lady his mate
To walk by their river side went.

He has turn'd and his seat he has ta'en
Behind yonder thick bushes rank ;
But he waiteth and waiteth in vain,
For they never return from the bank.

He gets up, puts his hand to his brow,
  Through his fingers directs he his sight,
But gone is the day with its glow,
  Come on in grey mantle the night.

Till long after sunset he stays,
  But when shone the small stars in the sky,
He mov'd to the water apace
  And began as was usual to cry.

O God, what new prospect is here,
  Sure hell has its power employ'd !
Where once flow'd the rivulet clear
  Are dry sand and a horrible void.

On the shore in confusion most great
  Rich garments are scatter'd around ;
Of the Lord and the Lady his mate
  Can no other traces be found.

It is true from the channel a rock
  Stretches up tow'rds heaven's deep blue ;
Surprisingly human that look
  Presenting two forms to the view !

Astonish'd that servant stood fast,
  Despair has seiz'd wholly his mind,
An hour and another is past
  Ere the use of his speech he could find.

' Krysia, O Krysia,' he cried,
  And Echo gave ' Krysia ' back ;
But nothing but echo replied,
  Nothing rose from the chasm so black.

He looks at the gulf and the rock,
   Cold sweat from his pallid face sprung,
His hoary head three times he shook,
   Would speak, but he holdeth his tongue.

He takes the dear child out with care,
   A smile of strange meaning he gives,
And murmuring devoutly a prayer,
   Returns to the cot where he lives.

THE FATHER'S RETURN

'Go, O children, go for the last time
To the place under the pillar on the mountain,
There before the miraculous image kneeling
Repeat piously the paternoster.

'The father does not return; morning and evening
In tears I have awaited and trouble.
The rivers are swollen, full of wild beasts the forests,
And the roads are full of robbers.'

The little children hear and run for the last time
To the place under the pillar on the mountain,
There they kneel before the miraculous image
And begin telling their rosaries.

They kiss the ground, after that, 'In the name of the Father,
Son and the Holy Ghost
Be glorified, and Holy Trinity
Now and at all times.'

After that—Our Father, the Ave and the Belief,
The Commandments and the Rose Crown,
And when they have entirely completed their beads
They take books out of their pockets.

And the Litany to the most Holy Mother
The elder brother sings, and with the brother
‘ O Holy Mother,’ add the children,
‘ Have mercy, have mercy, upon my father.’

But they hear the cracking of a whip, a wagon comes along the road,
And they know the wagon by its front ;
The children spring up and cry as loud as they can,
‘ Our father, O our father comes ! ’

The merchant looks, tears of joy he sheds,
He springs out of the wagon upon the ground :
‘ Ha ! what is the trouble, what has happened to you ?
Were you longing for your father ?

‘ Is your mother well ? your aunt ? the servants ?
But there you have currants in the basket ! ’
This he says to himself, and this he says to himself,
Full of pleasure and with much cry.

‘ Get on,’ the merchant cries to his servant,
‘ I shall walk with the children to the town.’
Quick, but lo, robbers gather around,
And the robbers are twelve in number.

Their beards are long, twisted their moustaches,
Their countenances wild, their garments dirty ;
Knives at their girdles, the swords at their sides gleam,
In their hands enormous clubs.

The children shriek, and fly to their father,
And lean under his mantle against his loins;
The servant trembles, the master becomes pale with fear,
Trembling he lifts up to the robbers his palms.

'O take the wagon, take the property,
Only leave us alive,
Do not make the little children orphans,
The young wife a widow.'

The band listens not, this already unharnesses the wagon,
Takes away the horses, but another
Cries 'Money,' and brandishes his club,
He with a sword falls upon the servant.

But 'Stop, stop!' cries the oldest robber,
And drives the band out of the road,
And delivering the children and the father,
'Go,' he said, 'away without fear.'

The merchant thanks him, but the robber replies,
'Don't thank me; I avow to thee frankly
I would have been the first to knock you on the head with my club
But for the rosary of the child.

'The children brought about that you have all escaped,
And that you are granted life and are uninjured;
Thank them for that which has been,
And how it has been I will tell you.

'For a long time we have heard of the coming of the merchant,
I and my comrades were in this place;
Near the top of the hill by the pillar
We placed ourselves on the watch.

'To-day, being here, and looking from under the bushes
The children prayed to God.
I heard, at first empty laughter seized me,
And then compassion and fear.

'I heard—the religion of my fathers came to my mind,
The club fell from my hand.
O, I have a wife, and with my wife
There are children young.

'Merchant, repair to the town, I must go to the wood,
And children, on this hill
Come occasionally, and for my soul
Pray a paternoster.'

CONRAD WALLENROD

(*A Fragment*)

To praise he listen'd with a heedless ear,
On beauty's face a distant glance he cast
And from enchanting prattle fled aghast.
Was he by nature dull and feelingless,
Was he from age ? He yet was young, I trow,
But he had wither'd cheeks and hair of snow,
The marks of ancient suffering and distress.
A mystery he in all. There times occurr'd
In which the sports of youth he blythe beheld,
Even with kindness female babble heard,
And graceful railleries with the like repell'd,
And dealt to courtly dames sweet words withal
With a cold smile, like plums to babies small.
There were rare moments of forgetfulness,
And presently the most indifferent word,
To all the rest which sounded meaningless,
In him a passionate emotion stirr'd ;
Such words as ' Lithuania,' ' wedded wife,'
' Duty,' ' crusade,' and ' fatherland ' were rife
To Conrad's bliss with poison the most fell.
These heard, anew averted he his eye,
An eye to all become insensible,
And plung'd himself in haughty mystery.
Perchance he 'd call'd to mind his stern employ
And his renouncement of all earthly joy.

He knew but one delight, 'twas friendship's tie;
With one man he in closest friendship trod,
A man of ghostly station, virtuous fame;
A grey monk, who of Halban bore the name,
Shar'd in the solitude of Wallenrod;
He was his soul's confessor good and kind,
He was the man who knew his inmost mind.
Blest friendship! sure a saint on earth he'll be,
Who has learnt to blend with friendship sanctity.

'Twas thus the Council of the Order weigh'd
Of Conrad Wallenrod the qualities;
But he had faults—and who without is made?
Conrad no worldly vanities did prize,
Ne'er willingly at drunken banquets stay'd;
Yet ne'ertheless, shut in his private bower,
When pain tormented him in any wise,
He solace sought in drinks of fiery power;
Then a new face he donn'd, as 'twould appear;
His visage, whilom pallid and severe,
Was colour'd with a certain sickly red;
And those great eyes, whilom of azure gaze,
Which mostly nothing saw and nothing said,
Of ancient fires launch'd forth the lightning rays:
Then mournful sighs from out his bosom gush'd,
And pearly teardrops to his eyelids rush'd;
His lute he seizes—from his mouth there flow
Strains in a language foreign and unknown;
But ah! the hearers well the import know,
They glean it from the music's funeral tone,
'Bove all they glean it from the songster's look.

Upon his features memory's stretch is shown,
Brows lifted, aspect downward bent, as though
He'll call up something from earth's deepmost nook;
Surely his song has some reality ;
Surely he thinks, and in half-faulty chase
His vanish'd youth he seeketh to retrace—
His soul the while in bounds of memory.

Never his hand in its harmonious round
Maketh the lute with tones of joy to sound.
Upon his face no smiles are seen to sport,
Forbid as were they sins of blackest sort.
With every chord he 's in sucession dealing,
Except alone the chord of joy which speaks ;
With yonder lute each feeling he awakes,
Save hope alone, worth every other feeling.

If unexpectedly on his retreat
The brothers come, a welcome strange they meet ;
As if awoke from sleep he starts : away
He casts his lute and stops his mournful lay ;
With a loud voice breathes horrid imprecations,
Addresses Halban in a whispering tone ;
Screams to the soldiers at the neighbouring stations
And threatens awfully some one unknown :
The brothers stand aghast, but Halban old
Sits and directs a glance so stern and cold
Upon his pupil's troubled countenance—
Full of mysterious meaning is that glance.
Does it remind him of some thing momentous ?
Does it in Conrad's heart awake dismay ?
Forthwith his forehead clears, its fire portentous
Loses his eye—his face grows cold as clay.

SYDOR KARPOWITCH

'My Lord and Master Sydor Karpowitch,
How many years to live art thou destin'd?'
'Seventy years, O motherkin, seventy years,
Seventy years, Pakomovna, seventy years.'

'My Lord and Master Sydor Karpowitch,
I fain would know the day thou wilt die on.'
'A Wednesday, O motherkin, a Wednesday,
A Wednesday, Pakomovna, a Wednesday.'

'My Lord and Master Sydor Karpowitch,
I fain would know the day of thy burial.'
'A Friday, O motherkin, a Friday,
A Friday, Pakomovna, a Friday.'

'My Lord and Master Sydor Karpowitch,
What day shall we hold thy funeral dinner?'
'A Saturday, O motherkin, a Saturday,
A Saturday, Pakomovna, a Saturday.'

'My Lord and Master Sydor Karpowitch,
Of what shall consist the funeral dinner?'
'Of pancakes, O motherkin, of pancakes,
Of pancakes, Pakomovna, of pancakes.'

'My Lord and Master Sydor Karpowitch,
Thy mournful knell on what shall we ring it?'
  'The frying pan, O motherkin, the frying pan,
  The frying pan, Pakomovna, the frying pan.'

'My Lord and Master Sydor Karpowitch,
Behind thee wilt thou leave many children?'
  'Seven children, motherkin, seven children,
  Seven children, Pakomovna, seven children.'

'My Lord and Master Sydor Karpowitch,
Wilt thou leave aught wherewith I may feed them?'
  'The wide world, O motherkin, the wide world,
  The wide world, Pakomovna, the wide world.'

'My Lord and Master Sydor Karpowitch,
How now should they roam the world in winter?'
  'In shoes of bark, O motherkin, in shoes of bark,
  In shoes of bark, Pakomovna, in shoes of bark.'

'My Lord and Master Sydor Karpowitch,
From teeth of dogs how shall they guard them?'
  'With cudgels, O motherkin, with cudgels,
  With cudgels, Pakomovna, with cudgels.'

'My Lord and Master Sydor Karpowitch,
In what shall they stow away their booty?'
  'In knapsacks, O motherkin, in knapsacks,
  In knapsacks, Pakomovna, in knapsacks.'

RYSLAN AND TCHORNOMOR [1]

But let us return to our hero—
Is it not disgraceful that we have so long occupied
ourselves
With a cap and with a beard
Leaving Ryslan to his fate ?
After finishing the dreadful combat with Rogdai
He rode through a thick wood ;
Before him appeared a wide valley
By the light of the morning heavens ;
The knight trembles against his will :
He sees an old battlefield,
Afar all is empty ; here and there
Bones are turning yellow ; on the hills
Are scattered quivers, coats of mail ;
Here is armour, here rusty spear ;
Here lies the sword in the bones of the hand ;
There is the . . . helm covered with grass
And the old skull mouldering in it,
There the whole skeleton of a warrior
With his trusty horse
Lies without motion ; spears, arrows,
Are buried in the dry earth,
And peaceful ivy covers them . . .

[1] There are two versions of this, neither of them complete. I have combined them to give a consecutive narrative.—[Ed.]

Nothing disturbs the voiceless quiet
Of this desert,
And the sun in its bright altitude
Illumines the valley of death.

With a sigh the hero looked round him
With melancholy eyes.
'O field, O field, who sowed thee
With dead corses?
What swift horse spurned thee
In the last hour of bloody battle?
Who upon thee fell with glory?
Whose prayers were heard by heaven?
Why, O field, art thou silent
And covered with the grass of forgetfulness? . . .
Perhaps there may be a time
When there will be no salvation to me from eternal obscurity!
It may be that on the hill of silence
Will stand the silent grave of the Ryslans
And the loud strain of the Baians
Will not speak of it.'

But quickly our hero remembered
That a good sword is necessary to a hero
And likewise mail; and the hero
Was unarmed from his last combat.
He goes around the field,
And seeks armour for himself
In the bushes, amongst the forgotten bones,
The coats of mail mouldering in heaps,
And the broken swords and helms.
Awaketh echo and also the dumb steppe,

Clash and noise are heard in the field ;
He takes up a lance, without making a choice,
He likewise finds a helm and a clear sounding horn,
But he can hardly discover a sword.
Going about the valley of slaughter
He sees a quantity of swords,
But they are all light, and too small,
And the prince was not a withered coxcomb,
Not like a knight of our days.
However, that he might have something to
Play with and avoid ennui,
He takes a steel spear in his hand,
He puts a coat of mail
Upon his breast,
And proceeds farther on his journey.

Already palens the vermilion,
Over the sleeping earth
The grey mist reeks
And the yellow moon uprises,
The steppe becomes dusky. Along the dark path
Buried in oblivion goes our Ryslan,
And sees through the nocturnal mist
A huge hill blackening afar off
From which seems to proceed an awful snoring.
He approaches nearer and nearer to the hill and listens.
The wonder hill appears as if it breathes.
Ryslan pays heed and looks
Without being terrified and with a tranquil soul ;

But agitated, with affrighted ear,
The horse resists, shudders,
Trembles with obstinate head,
And erects his mane stiff.[1]

But now the hill illumin'd by
The moon, no longer overcast
By clouds, distinct appears at last,
And the knight sees—O how shall I
Find words to paint what he beheld ?—
A living head stood him before,
The monstrous eyes by slumber seal'd ;
It snores, and at each awful snore
It mov'd the helmet which it wore,
Causing the plumes the helmet bore
Take shades to wave on high
In grand terrific majesty.
O'er the dark steppe the head did tower,
By silence compass'd wide about ;
The senseless guardian of the place,
It stands before our Ryslan stout,
A terrible and misty mass.
The knight, in doubt what means to take
The head's mysterious sleep to break,
Round it rides repeatedly,
Viewing it with attentive glance,
Till before the snout pausing he
Tickles the nostrils with his lance.
Writhing a yawn the head he sees ;
The eyes it opens, it gives a sneeze,

[1] Here begins the second version, which is rimed.—[Ed.]

A whirlwind rises bending tree
And tossing dust-clouds to the sky.
Startled by the dreadful sound,
From brows, moustache and eyelids, bound
Owls in flocks, the rocks around
Are waken'd—Echo sneezes high.
Disdainful back look'd Ryslan bold,
As he with rein his courser stay'd,
Then answer'd haughtily and cold,
' What wouldst thou say to me, Sir Head ? '
' Why, this have I to say to thee,'
Replied the head in accents gruff,
' Though Fate sends thee as guest to me,
'Tis night, I wish to sleep, pack off ! '
But the brave warrior when he heard
The monster bluster at this rate
Replied, with sudden anger stirr'd,
' Be still, be still, O empty pate,
'Tis a true saying, I will maintain,
Broad brow and little brain ;
I 'll gallop, I 'll gallop and galloping whistle,
And for nobody care a thistle.'
Then dumb with rage the head became
And swoll'n with hatred's pent-up flame.
The blood-shot eyes were all aglow,
From mouth and ears and nostrils broke
A stifling cloud of mist and smoke ;
Then suddenly it began to blow
With all its fury, all its might,
A whirlwind 'gainst our worthy knight.
In vain the horse with close shut eyes
His head downward, bosom straining, through
Whirlwind and rain and darkness tries

His forward journey to pursue,
And bear his lord like courser tried
To regions where less danger lies.
Wilder'd, confus'd, he stops and sighs—
Around to wheel and brave the wind
The warrior strives repeatedly ;
Vainly, vainly, whilst behind
Laugheth the head with maniac glee,
Thund'ring, ' O stay, my gallant, stay !
Sir knight, you break your neck in vain,
Tarry, my cockrel of the main,
Show no white feather, stay, knight, stay !
Surely you 'd scorn to run away ;
Rejoice my heart with a single blow,
Ere horse and man to the devil go.'
Then he mocks the knight with frightful tongue,
Ryslan to the heart though stung,
No reply by language makes,
But his lance he vengeful shakes,
And the steel by his good hand flung
Pierces deep the daring tongue,
Causing from the yawning throat
Blood to gush in torrents out ;
Then losing its bold bearing quite
And all desire to rave and rail,
The head stares wond'ring at the knight,
Biteth the iron and turns pale.
As on our stage we sometimes see
A pupil of Melpomene,
A stupid dolt he may be call'd,
Check'd by the unexpected hiss,
Doth suddenly his vapouring dismiss
And stammering, speechless, stand appall'd,

The scorn and laughter of the crowd,
So stands that head, of late so proud.
Profiting by the panic dread,
O'ercome with which he saw the head,
Like lightning forward Ryslan sprang
And with his good hand gauntleted
Struck on the cheek that monster head
A blow which through the desert rang.
Then did the dewy grass become
Empurpled round with bloody foam ;
Then was the grass around so wide
With blood and foam commingled dyed.
The head is tottering, turning round,
It falls, once steadfast as a rock,
The molten helm the earth doth knock,
And upon the now abandon'd ground
Began to gleam a war-sword broad and bright.
The head it totters and turns round,
It falls and welters on the ground,
And in its place in the moonlight
There lay a war-sword broad and bright.
Our knight, delighted at the sight,
Seizes upon the glittering prize,
And then with fury in his eyes
Back to the head he swiftly goes,
Bent to cut off its ears and nose.
But sudden with surprise he hears
The head a piteous groan pronounce,
And when that moan salutes his ears,
He drops the lifted sword at once.
For how can hero hew with steel,
When cries the vanquished ' Spare, O spare ? '
And how can hero anger feel,

When wretchedness breathes forth its
prayer ?
At that poor sob all vengeance soon
And lust for further vengeance dies,
As in the valley thaws the ice
Before the genial heat of noon.
'Thou 'st taught me, hero young and strong,'
Exclaim'd the head with a deep sigh,
'By means of thy good hand that I
In this dispute have done thee wrong;
Subject to thee henceforth am I,
But, knight, show magnanimity.
My fate deserves the pitying tear,
As you 'll confess, when it you hear.
I too was once a warrior, know!
A warrior too I 've been, Sir Knight.
Triumphant, proud, I trod the ground,
But in a younger brother found
A foe who was my bane and blight;
The crafty, treacherous Tchornomor,
Of all our race the scoff and scorn,
A cursed dwarf with gray beard born,
Was source of all my miseries sore.
The wretch could not without annoy
Upon my wondrous stature gaze;
Therefore to harm me was his joy
From his bad boyhood's early days.
Though enormous was my stature,
Though incredible my vigour,
Rather simple was my nature,
Whilst, though contemptible of figure,
This vile, detestable deceiver
Was as clever, quite as clever,

As the very, very devil,
And in all respects as evil.
Moreover in his beard of gray
Concealed much fatal strength there lay,
So that the whole world he disdain'd,
For well he knew that he was safe
However foes might rage and chafe,
Whilst that gray beard intact remain'd.

Once with a very friendly face,
'Brother,' he said, 'I have to beg of thee,
Brother, a deed of especial grace:
I hope you 'll not refuse it me.
In my dark books of grammarye
I 've read that by a lonely shore,
Beyond the eastern mountains high
In a deep vault with huge locks four,
Is hid a sword and, what think'st thou?
How shall I tell the tidings now?
This sword, this sword, this fatal sword,
As I from a strange mirror know,
Which future things disclos'd to me,
Is doom'd by hostile destiny,
(Who ever thing more horrid heard?)
To cut thy head off and my beard.[1]

Judge yourself
How necessary it is for us to get possession
Of this the creation of evil spirits!
'Well, where is the difficulty?'

[1] Here the first version is resumed.—[Ed.]

Said I to the dwarf, ' I am ready,
I will go, though to the end of the world.'
I cast a pine on one shoulder
And on the other for counsel
Placed my evil brother ;
I set out for the distant journey,
I strode, I strode, and, glory to God,
Although the prophecies were for evil,
All turned out prosperously at first.
Behind the distant mountains
We found the vault of destiny ;
I ransacked it with my hands,
And obtained the concealed sword.
But no ! fate wished for that :
Between us a dispute arose—
And it was, I avow, on this account !
The question : who should have the sword ?
I disputed, the dwarf became angry ;
We quarrelled long ; at last
The cunning one imagined a guile,
It appeared as if he was becoming tender.
' Let us leave profitless dispute,'
Said to me earnestly Tchornomor,
' By it we weaken our alliance ;
Reason advises us to live in peace ;
Let us permit fate to decide
To whom this sword shall belong.
Let us bend both our ears to the ground
(What wickedness did he not imagine !)
And he who first hears a sound
He shall possess the sword until his grave.'
He said, and laid himself down on the earth ;
I had grown such a fool, I also stretched myself out.

'I shall lie,' said I, smiling, 'shall hear nothing,
And will deceive him!'
But deceived myself terribly.
The wretch with the greatest silence,
Rising, came behind me on tiptoes,
Brandished the sword;
Like a whirlwind whistled the sharp blade,
And before I could look around me,
Already my head flew from my shoulders,
And supernatural force
Retained in it the spirit of life.
My skeleton is overgrown with thorns;
Far in a country, forgotten by people,
Corrupts my unburied dust.[1]

But to this region wild and lone
Wafted the warlock wretched me,
That I should stand for ever guard
Over the dreadful magic sword
This day thy valour won for thee.
Take it, and may God with thee go!
Now shouldst thou 'midst thy wanderings meet
By any chance the dwarfish foe,
I hope the wretch thou 'lt fitly greet
For all his craft and cruelty.
Then I at length should happy be
And tranquilly should cease to live,
And in my gratitude forgive
The buffet which thou gavest me.'

[1] Here the rimed version is resumed.—[Ed.]

THE TURKS AT EGER

At summoning the city the Turks were not slack,
Good use of all kinds of languages quickly they
make,
In Hungarian and German and Latin they clack,
In Polish, Slavonian and savage Walack,

And thus their words sounded as borne through
the air:
'By the beard of the Prophet the Pasha doth swear,
If ye to the Sultan will yield up Eger,
He'll dismiss ye all free with rich presents and rare.'

Black Istvan ear from a loophole has lent,
With some of his comrades to council he went,
And unto his purpose their minds he so bent,
That to yield up the city they freely consent.

Black Istvan Hegedus spoke to his rout:
'To Governor Dobo for siege money shout,
And if he'll give ye none from the city march out;
The Turk will perform all his promise, no doubt.'

But the Governor Dobo of this treason soon heard,
And summoning Metzkei who command with him
shar'd
Sir Hegedus straight they commit to safe ward,
Where tortur'd by water his guilt he declar'd.

In the market erect they three gallowses tall,
And according to language the traitors hung all,
And their heads chopping off them on poles they install,
And to Hegedus' office one Imre they call.

What a shame it had been, what a source of dismay,
Had Hegedus barter'd fair Eger away;
Then the country around had become the Turks' prey,
And been lost to the Christian for ever and aye.

THE FALL OF ZOLNOK

Bernald, who the rural affairs was plac'd o'er,
Aldanai Bernald, a warrior of power,
On hearing of Temesvar's downfall so sore,
Has Lippa abandon'd and Solymos tower.

Great Akmet the Pasha could scarce understand
How places like these could fall into his hand,
With vivers provided and cannons so grand,
And plenty of florins from King Ferdinand.

Then Ali of Buda and great Akmet are
Encourag'd and say: 'We will push on our war
To Zolnok and Eger, less trouble by far
They 'll cost us to take them than did Temesvar.'

So Akmet the Pasha to Zolnok has ta'en
His way, him with troops twenty thousand amain
Ali Pasha precedes, and with cannon a train
The city was batter'd a week but in vain.

Bold Lorentz Nyari was Governor there,
With seven hundred soldiers all proper men fair,
But alas! they of different languages were,
So that all was dissension and trouble and care.

Of cannons and mortars there were twenty-four
In Zolnok, of sakers a thousand and more,
Fifteen hundred muskets from Biscay brought o'er,
Nine hundred pood weight of good powder in store ;

There were firearms in plenty, much iron and tin
And gold, which had late in the royal chest been,
But, alack ! all was captur'd the city within.
Yet how could a foeman hope Zolnok to win ?

O mighty was Zolnok and beauteous, I trow,
On one side the Tisza its current did show,
On the other Zagiva did murmuring flow,
Uniting together the city below.

On the side of the North was a trench deep and wide,
Three bastions stood up at three corners in pride ;
Huge ramparts the place of high walls well supplied,
The house-tops behind them could scarce be descried.

Now Akmet the Pasha, so stern and so dread,
Before Zolnok town his appearance has made ;
Upon the green plain he his army has stay'd,
His camp he has pitch'd and his banner display'd.

What tumult and noise from that campment arise :
Bells rang, cymbals clang, amid thousand wild cries ;

Fifes squeak, the drums speak, trumpets shriek
to the skies ;
Of the great host the ends can't be scann'd by
the eyes.

The sight and the sounds to the townsmen recall
Losontzi's destruction and Temesvar's fall ;
There 's whispering and murmuring amongst
great and small ;
The power of the Sultan their minds doth appal.

At length they resolve from the city to fly,
They thought if they stay'd, by the Turks they
should die ;
On the fourth of September when midnight was
nigh,
They depart, without bidding their leader good-bye.

Full quickly Nyari Laurentius knew
That Zolnok was left by his soldiers untrue ;
All alone he remain'd ; what alone can he do ?
They clos'd not the gate, when from Zolnok they
flew.

Long doubtful he stood in unspeakable woe ;
Should he follow the fugitive traitors ? ah no !
Far better be slain by the hands of the foe,
Than to live a disgrace and become a vile show.

Around he speeds to the city's wide gate,
Determin'd on death, for his courage was great ;
'Twas dawn and the drum of [the] Turks loudly
beat,
They knew not that Zolnok was left to its fate.

But as they came onward in order of fight,
A huge burst of smoke from the town met their sight.
They guess'd that its soldiers had left it outright,
And they push'd for the entrance as fast as they might.

In the gate of the city bold Lorentz did stand,
Alone he withstood them with terrible brand,
Many Turks he dispatch'd ere they master'd his hand—
O, woe to his dastardly runaway band!

How glad were the Pashas I scarcely need tell,
In the hands of the Sultan when fair Zolnok fell;
To the clouds in their joy ' Allah, Allah,' they yell,
In the town they found store of all things they lik'd well.

In Colosvar city these lines compos'd I,
Sebastian Tinodi in great misery,
Blowing on my nails in a cold chamber high,
For want of a penny some fuel to buy.

THE DEATH OF YOTI

I BETIMES got up, full two hours before day-break,
I for water call to wash me and that I may feel
awake.
A storm 's raging in the forest, creak the oaks, the
pines give way,
Loud the Klephts abuse their captain for the
smallness of their pay.
'Why art up so early, Yoti? better whilst thou
canst repose.'
'Soon the Pagans will attack us, they hemming us
enclose.'
'Hold your tongue, you silly fellow, what hast
got into thy head?'
'For my cursed wounds bring med'cine. O,
remove the stinging lead!
Pull me up if you are able and support me whilst
I sit,
Bring me wine, sweet wine of power, I 'd sit and
drink a bit,
So that I may sing old ballads, ballads such as
make one cry—
O that I were on the mountains 'mid thick shades
on mountains high!
Where the little lambs are bounding and the fat
sheep dozing lie!'

SKULLODEMOS

SKULLODEMOS is sit[t]ing eating in the pine tree,
And he has Eirenie at his side to pour out wine for him ;
' Pour out for me, lovely Eirenie, until it becomes light,
Till the morning star arises that the birds may have their breakfast,
When I will send thee home with ten cupbearers.'
' Demos, I am not a servant that I should pour out wine for you,
I am the betrothed of Proestos and the daughter of the governor Archontos.'
At the dawn of morn two travellers come unto him
And they have long beards and black faces,
And the two standing near to him salute him :
' Good day to you, Demos mine.'—' A good day to you, travellers !
How do you know that I am Skullodemos ? '
' We bear greetings to you from your brother ? '
' Travel[l]ers ! Where did you know my brother ? '
' In Yanina, in the prison, we saw him confin'd.
He had irons on his hands and his feet were in the stocks.'
And Skullodemos wept and made a motion to flee.
' Where do you go, O Demos, my brother, where do you go, O captain ?

Thy brother is here, come let me kiss you.'
And he knew him and seized him in his arms
And the two sweetly kissed each other in the eyes and the lips
And then Demos asked him and said :
' How, my sweet brother, did you come to us ?
How did you deliver your hands from the Albanians ? '
' At night I freed my hands and broke the stocks
And broke the chains and leaped into the morass,
And I found a one-oared boat and crossed the lake.
The day before yesterday I left Yanina and gained the mountain.'

PLIAZKA

Pliazka is lying in the desert spring,
With his feet in the water but he still craveth for more :
With the birds he holds discourse and with the swallows :
'Is there a chance, little bird, that I get better,
A chance, little bird, of my cure ?'
'Dear Pliazka, if you wish for a remedy and to have your wounds cured,
Mount high into Olympos into the beautiful region,
The brave there are not sick, and the sick there become brave,
There are the many Klephts, the four first,
There share the money and the capitancy ;
The Potamia belongs to Nikos, the Alason to Kristos,
Tolios the present year is captain in Caterina,
And the leper Lazopulon has for his lot Platamona.'
And the unfortunate, ever unfortunate Pliazka
Went down into Tournato to divert himself there,
And the enemies following him, cut of[f] his head.

YANNES STATHA

A BLACK bark its course is steering by Casandra's lovely shore,
Black was every sail it carried, black the ensign which it bore,
Tow'rds it comes a Turkish corvette: 'Strike your sails or down ye go.'
'I 'll not strike a sail before ye, I 'll no craven spirit show.
Do not hope to daunt a bridegroom hastening to the bridal hall,
Yannes I, Statha by surname, son-in-law of Poukoval.
My boys, display your mettle, fiercely at the corvette drive,
Board at once, and then no quarter, leave no pagan dog alive.'
Broken with the dread encounter was the Turkman's lofty prow,
Yannes was the first to board him, sword in hand, and strike a blow.
Ran with Turkish blood the scuppers, till the sea around was dyed,
On the deck themselves down flinging, 'Allah! Allah!' the Turks cried.

THE DREAM OF DEMOS

NOT once nor five times even have I to Demos said:
'Go not so bravely dress'd about, nor with so high a head.
The Albanians all thy steps are dogging and are eager thee to slay,
To chastise thy proud behaviour and make thy gold their prey.'
The cuckoos speak it in the mountains, the partridges upon the plain,
A little, little bird doth speak it into the chieftain's startled brain;
But not in speech of birds 'tis spoken,
Not that which we from swallows hear,
But 'tis in speech of mortals spoken, in human language plain and clear.
'Why, Demos mine, art thou so pallid? Why cover'd o'er with cobwebs grey?'
'Since, pretty little bird, you ask me, to you the whole truth I will say.
I stepp'd aside behind the arras, now, little bird, the truth I tell,
And as I slept behind the arras, for in a troubled sleep I fell,
I saw the heaven all beblooded, beblooded were the stars, I ween,
Beblooded too was my trusty sabre, my trusty sabre Damascene.'

POUKOVAL

WHAT is all this fell disturbance, what this tumult near and far,
Is it buffaloes being slaughter'd, is it wild beasts waging war ?
'Tis not buffaloes being slaughter'd, 'tis not wild beasts waging war,
It is Poukoval that 's fighting with the Turks both near and far,
With ten thousand savage Turkmen he is engag'd in desperate fray,
From Kerasoo of the hillock down unto Kanouria's bay.
From a window cries a damsel with long hair so bright and fine,
' Stop, O Yannes, stop the fighting, cease to ply that gun of thine
Till the clouds of dust may settle, and o'er is the hur[r]icane,
So that we may count how many yet survive of thy good train.'
Three times are the Turkmen number'd, just three hundred still survive,
Only once the Klephts are number'd, only three remain alive.
One is gone in quest of water, one is gone in search of bread,
Whilst the third, the tallest, fairest, gun on shoulder, proudly stay'd.

KALIAKONDI

WOULD that I were a bird that I might fly, that I might go
And look to the Franks on the island of unfortunate Ithaka!
That I might hear Loukaina, the wife of Louke!
How she mourns and sheds black tears;
As the partridge afflicts herself how she strips off her locks,
Like the feathers of the crows—she has all her dress;
At the window she sits and looks at the sea,
And as many ships as pass she puts question to:
'Ships, my vessels, my golden brigantines,
Ye who speed and come into the desert Baltos,
Do ye know my husband Louke Kaliakondi?
We left him yesterday in Zaurolin,
He was seated with a joint of lamb, had mutton on the spit,
And five prisoners were turning the spits,
They had lamb and were supping.
A young lamb was cooking for him on a spit,
He on a loin of lamb was feasting, before the fire did roast a sheep,
Whilst five Wallachian captive lasses the pitchfork spit did turning keep.

THE ENGLISH GYPSY

He

As I to the town was going one day
My Roman lass I met by the way.
Said I, 'Young maid, will you share my lot?'
Said she, 'Another wife you 've got.'
'Ah, no!' to my Roman lass I cried,
'No wife have I in the world so wide;
And you my wedded wife shall be,
If you will consent to come with me.'

She

As I to the town was going one day
I met a young Roman upon the way.
Said he, 'Young maid, will you share my lot?'
Said I, 'Another wife you 've got.'
'No, no!' the handsome young Roman cried,
'No wife have I in the world so wide;
And you my wedded wife shall be,
If you will share my lot with me.'

HUNGARIAN GYPSY SONG

To the mountain the fowler has taken his way,
There he doth eat and make himself gay
From the basket thou bearest thy shoulder upon;
Thou art the fowler's gay leman, I ween,
Who rovest with him in the mountain so green—
Bearing the basket thy shoulder upon.

A SPANISH GYPSY BALLAD

UNTO a refuge me they led
To save from dungeon drear ;
Then sighing to my wife I said :
' I leave my baby dear.'

Back from the refuge soon I sped
My child's sweet face to see ;
Then sternly to my wife I said :
' You 've seen the last of me.'

O, when I sit my courser bold,
My bantling in my rear,
And in my hand my musket hold,
O how they quake with fear.

Pray, little baby, pray the Lord,
Since guiltless still thou art,
That peace and comfort He afford
To this poor troubled heart.

False Hoaniho, day and night,
Had best with caution go ;
The Gypsy carles of Yeira height
Have sworn to lay him low.

Nine years are past since this abode
  Thou left'st to grief a prey,
And took'st to Christ the heavenward road,
  To Him account to pay.

Upon the King may evils pour!
  Such ills from him I 've borne;
From me my parents lov'd he tore—
  I now am left forlorn.

Within a garden rav'd and yell'd
  A desperate robber horde,
And in their hands they muskets held
  To shoot their God and Lord.

There rov'd a swine by yonder wood,
  A paper at its ear,
And on that paper written stood:
  'Come, take me, Gypsy dear.'

I wash'd not in the limpid flood
  The shirt which binds my frame;
In Hoaniho Ralli's blood
  I bravely wash'd the same.

I sallied forth upon my grey
  With him my hated foe,
And when we reach'd the narrow way
  I dealt a dagger blow.

I have a gallant mare in stall;
  My mother gave that mare,
That I might seek Count Pepé's hall
  And steal his son and heir.

I slouch my beaver o'er my brow,
  As down the street I rove,
For fear thy mother keen should know
  That I her daughter love.

The thistle-weed thou must not sow,
  If thou wouldst fruit obtain ;
As poor would be the garden's show,
  As would the gardener's gain.

I for a cup of water cried,
  But they refus'd my pray'r ;
Then straight into the road I hied
  And fell to robbing there.

I ask'd for fire to warm my frame,
  But they 'd have scorn'd my pray'r,
If I, to pay them for the same,
  Had stript my body bare.

Away, Count Pepé, seek the hill,
  To flee 's the only chance ;
With bayonets fixt, thy blood to spill,
  See soldiers four advance.

The Gypsy-fiend of Manga mead,
  Who never gave a straw,
He would destroy for very greed
  The good Egyptian law.

I walk'd the street and there I spied
  A goodly gallows-tree,
And in my ear methought it cried :
  'Gypsy ! beware of me !'

The Church I enter'd, thither bound
  With God discourse to hold,
And when I left it, lo! I found—
  A prize—five crowns of gold.

I bounded through my cottage door
  My partner to embrace,
And lo! I found her weeping o'er
  My dying infant's face.

I spurr'd my courser o'er the ford,
  Afar my luck I'd try—
Encounter'd me my God and Lord
  And said: 'Where dost thou hie?'

There came a scanty Gypsy train
  Adown the village street,
Who with their children did complain
  That they had nought to eat.

And when they found their tears and cries
  No charity could wring,
To heaven they rais'd their ghastly eyes
  And curs'd its awful King.

I spoke, 'twas at the King's command,
  And as I spoke he smil'd
Benign, and now by all the land
  Your Highness I am styl'd.

There comes the Alcaide, and I am led
  To prison now away,
Because I plunder'd, as 'tis said,
  A house the other day.

An archer comes and through the fair
  He seeks a Gypsy now,
Because the farmers all declare
  That he has stole a sow.

The King in fear before me runs,
  Because I him would slay ;
He bears with him his little ones,
  Lest hands on them I lay.

Along the pathway as I trod,
  A beggar met my eye,
And at her cries the Almighty God
  Descended from on high.

O counsel, precious counsel, yield
  Sweet Jesus, in my need,
How I may get my jars refill'd,
  Myself and bairns to feed.

The priest of Villa Franca bold
  Proclaimeth far and wide,
That he the law which Gypsies hold
  Is bent to set aside.

And see, adown the road doth prance
  The priest in full array ;
In fear before his countenance
  Facundo runs away.

I left my house and walk'd about,
  They seiz'd me fast and bound.
' It is a Gypsy thief,' they shout,
  ' The Spaniards here have found.'

From out the prison me they led,
  Before the Scribe they brought.
'It is no Gypsy-thief,' he said,
  'The Spaniards here have caught.'

Throughout the night, the dusky night,
  I prowl in silence round,
And with my eyes look left and right
  For him, the Spanish hound,
That with my knife I him may smite
  And to the vitals wound.

The fools have said I stole their bed,
  Their words are all untrue ;
'Twas Spaniards bred, I 'll gage my head,
  For harm to none I do.

Will no one to the sister bear
  News of her brother's plight,
How in this cell of dark despair
  To cruel death he 's dight ?

We all are met, a sign I make
  That she abroad should steal,
For to yon maid my mind to break
  So sore inclin'd I feel.

She told me she would gladly wear
  A hat of Portugal ;
To-morrow's morn 'twill be my care
  To buy one at the stall.

The youth to execution went,
  Held fast by soldiers' hands,
The Queen proclaim'd him innocent,
  And freed him from his bands.

To far Madrid's fair town I walk'd
The gracious Queen to view,
And in my tongue to her I talk'd,
Like an Egyptian true.

Within the street they 're selling, see,
Of crystal vases fine ;
' Dear Mother, purchase one for me,
I 'll fill it up with wine.'

I hate a wife who sits at home,
A-fondling aye her child ;
Unto the brandy-shops I roam
And drink till I am wild.

To-morrow's morn comes grisly death,
From him the clothes to tear ;
Then cries his mother, out of breath,
' I 'll of the clothes take care ! '

I begging go o'er plain and hill,
Full dreary is my beat ;
Yet goodly alms I gather still
When I some ninny meet.

I saw, as midst the hills I stray'd,
The figure of the dead,
Which, with its lighted lamp display'd,
Did fill my heart with dread.

A wench for impudence renown'd
Approach'd a butcher's stall ;
Says she : ' I want of meat a pound,
But with no bone at all.'

To her the butcher answer made
  With utmost courtesy :
' When I, fair lass, the price am paid,
  I 'll hand the meat to thee.'

Along the road, along its side,
  The thieves in ambush lie,
And there they hide until shall ride
  My Lord the Colonel by.

And they with dagger and with knife
  A-plundering there are gone,
And they are bent to take his life,
  Because they food have none.

From out the prison me they bore,
  Upon an ass they plac'd,
And scourg'd me till I dripp'd with gore,
  As down the road it pac'd.

They bore me from the prison nook,
  They bade me rove at large ;
When out I 'd come a gun I took,
  And scath'd them with its charge.

From out Madrid I, wretch, have fled
  With many a tear and sigh,
Because the cruel King has said :
  ' This Gypsy, he shall die.'

Within his ingle sits at ease
  Each wealthy Gypsy churl,
Whilst all the needy ones they seize,
  And into prison hurl.

The King has issued a command,
  With much ado and pain,
That all the Gypsies of the land
  Shall live and not be slain.

My basket in my hand I took,
  To market I would go ;
I saw a blade of swarthy look
  And cried : ‘ A Gypsy, ho ! ’

Of Gypsy folk a scanty few
  Into the wood had stray’d,
But out in hurry soon they flew
  Before the fierce Alcaide.

I wrote a letter fair and white
  With much ado and pain ;
Then said the Queen, in wrath and spite :
  ‘ He ne’er shall freedom gain.’

They gave me bonny eggs in alms
  And them I soon devour’d ;
The whites which rose, with grievous qualms,
  My senses overpower’d.

Within a hut assembled were
  Of nobles not a few ;
And they were met and gather’d there
  That no one them might view.

My hat and mantle on I cast,
  To sally forth I thought,
Then by the greaves they seiz’d me fast
  And I my dagger caught.

The other day abroad I went
  Upon our Queen to look ;
And lo ! she sate and read intent
  The constitution-book.

My mule so bonny I bestrode,
  To Portugal I 'd flee,
And as I o'er the water rode
  A man came suddenly,
And he his love and kindness show'd,
  By setting his dog on me.

Roruntcho Lopez, gallant lad,
  A-smuggling he would ride ;
He stole his father's ambling prad,
  I therefore him must hide.

The thieves, the thieves are on the watch
  Amidst the hills so green—
They 're on the watch, that they may catch
  The money and the Queen.

There sate a lord of note and fame
  Within a lonely inn,
Then suddenly the thieves they came
  And stript him to the skin.

Towards my home I bent my course
  Then Death to me drew nigh,
'And where art bound ?' he bellow'd hoarse—
  'Home, home,' was my reply.

O, I will be no Gentleman,
  I 'm sprung from Gypsy tree ;
O, I am not of gentle clan
  But an Egyptian free.

O cease to talk in Romany,
  Ye Gypsy gallants twain,
For La Kartchofa here ye see
  Who understands your strain.

I 'm bitten by the frosty air,
  The fleas about me swarm ;
Unto the great house I 'll repair
  And there myself I 'll warm.

If down the street, my friend, thou stray
  And my dear wife thou meet ;
I 'm plying, say, the shears all day,
  That she the pot may heat.

I hasten home, but leave with thee
  A portion of my heart ;
For if thou home wilt come with me,
  I will the whole impart.

On high arose the moon so fair,
  The Gypsy 'gan to sing ;
I see a Spaniard coming there,
  I must be on the wing.

The night descends, yet I 'm afraid
  Abroad my face to show ;
I fear to meet a soldier blade,
  Who 'd kill me at a blow.

This house of harlotry doth smell,
  I flee as from the pest ;
Your mother likes my sire too well,
  To hie me home is best.

That lass with cheek of rosy hue,
  That 's entering now the gate,
She does not come to visit you,
  She comes on me to wait.

O daughter, hide thy breasts for shame ;
  For them the boy can see !
And if he can or cannot, Dame !
  He 's long been lov'd by me.

This night to dog the priest I go,
  And shed his priestly gore ;
Then I will haste myself to throw
  The Monarch's feet before.

The girl I love more dear than life
  Should other gallant woo,
I 'd straight unsheath my dudgeon knife
  And cut his weazand through,
Or he, the conqueror in the strife,
  The same to me should do.

The shoes, O girl, which thou dost bear
  On those white feet of thine,
To none resign for love or prayer—
  They 're bought with coin of mine.

The gallows grim they 've rais'd once more,
  The hangman ready stands ;
And all to kill a partridge poor,
  That 's fallen in their hands.

'Midst soldier now and Alguazil
  The culprit forth they bear ;
The tapers grace divine instil
  Above his head which flare.

Once on a time in bed when laid
  With her whom I adore,
When to caress her I essay'd
  She said : ' Thou fool, give o'er.'

Once on a time in bed when laid
  With that same lassie brave,
When to caress her I essay'd
  Both hand and lip she gave.

Within the street thou down hast lain
  To slumber in the ray,
And yonder comes the justice train
  Who 'll thee in prison lay.

To spy thy window, love, I go,
  For I would creep in there,
And out to thee thy things I 'd throw,
  Thy mother not aware.

I 'll rise to-morrow, bread to earn,
  For hunger's worn me grim,
And all I meet I 'll ask in turn,
  If they 've no beasts to trim.

The thieves waylaid and beat me sore
  As tow'rds Madrid I came ;
For I was bound to peach, they swore,
  And all their deeds proclaim.

The priest, when last to church I went,
  With reverend look drew near
And ask'd me when 'twas my intent
  The royal mass to hear.

The Gypsy bold himself enroll'd
  As soldier of the King ;
But he deserted with the gold
  And therefore he must swing.

Seek, seek the Church, thou 'st broke the law,
  The Alguazil I see ;
He comes on thee to set his claw
  And drag to custody.

I ran to Clunes judgment seat
  My forfeit life to crave ;
The judges rose upon their feet
  And chains and dungeon gave.

Across the market as I sped
  I chanc'd a corse to spy :
' That man is dead,' a woman said—
  And, faith ! she told no lie.

I come a-begging to your gate,
  A maim'd and crippled wight,
From out the prison thrust of late,
  In rags and tatters dight ;
May thy blest Saint from such a fate
  Protect thee, good Sir Knight !

I leave my home and haste to roam
  In yonder bark of pride ;
To lands far o'er the salt sea foam
  Where foreign nations bide.

In vest with silver buttons fraught
  There comes a cove so bold,
In jacket tight, so neatly wrought
  And girdle stuff'd with gold.[1]

I stole a plump and bonny fowl,
  But ere I 'd off it din'd,
The master came, with scowl and growl,
  And me would captive bind.

My boots upon my legs I drew,
  And scour'd across the lea,
Then cried the Devil, with loud halloo:
  'Where does the Gypsy flee?'

Loud sang the Spanish Cavalier,
  And thus his ditty ran:
'God send the Gypsy lassie here
  And not the Gypsy man!'

At midnight when the moon began
  To show her silver flame,
There came to him no Gypsy man,
  The Gypsy lassie came.

[1] MS. incomplete here.—[Ed.]

OUR HEART IS HEAVY, BROTHER

The strength of the ox,
The wit of the fox,
  And the leveret's speed ;
All, all to oppose
Their numerous foes
  The Romany need.

Our horses they take,
Our wagons they break,
  And us they seize
In their prisons to coop,
Where we pine and droop
  For want of breeze.

When the dead swallow
The fly shall follow
  Across the sea,
We 'll then forget
The wrongs we have met,
  And forgiving be——.
    Brother, of that be certain.

GYPSY SONG

Up, up, brothers,
  Cease your revels !
The Gentile 's coming—
  Run like devils.

I do not like your way of life
  Ye men of Christian creed ;
I 'd rather live the kind of life
  Which forest foxes lead.

THE GYPSY

The plains are thirsting after water, the lofty mountains snow desire,
The Christian priests are fond of pullets, the Turks the Christian dress admire.
What is the matter with the wretched Gypsy woman,
Who had the two sons and the third in the brother
And now is gone mad, and walks about, weeps,
Neither shows herself in the plains nor in the rugged mountains ?
She, they say, drags herself to the Wallachian sorcerers,
And there they fire at her out of the gun thunder,
And this they do not shoot in festivals nor marriages,
But they shoot at the Gypsy with lead in the knees and hands.
As a tree is torn up, as a young cypress flings itself here and there,
And with a loud voice, she cries to the youth whom they seek :
'Where are you my lovely brother, and dearest one,
Turn back to me, turn back to me your head from the field,
That black Yussuph and the pagans do not catch thee
And carry thee to Yanina to the dog Ali Pasha.'

THE GYPSY'S WELCOME TO THE NEW YEAR

Welcome to our tent, New Year!
We hope you come our hearts to cheer:
Goodness and good luck, come in!
Fly out, fly out, bad luck and sin!

THE GYPSY'S HOMELAND

The region of Tcha is our dear native soil,
Where in fulness of pleasure we liv'd without toil,
Till dispers'd through all lands 'twas our fortune
to be,
Tchai greis appiya la panee Loucallee.

Once Kings came from far to kneel down at our
gate,
And princes rejoic'd on our meanest to wait;
But now who so mean but would scorn our
degree?
Tchai greis appiya la panee Loucallee.

For the Ultebe saw from his throne in the cloud
That our deeds they were foolish, our hearts they
were proud,
And in anger he bade us his presence to flee—
Tchai greis appiya la panee Loucallee.

Our steeds of no river should drink but of one,
It sparkles through Tcha 'neath the smile of the
sun,
But they taste of all streams save that only and
see—
Tchai greis appiya la panee Loucallee.

GYPSY SCENES

O WIFE, beseech the prison lord
  That he this chain remove,
For I shall perish overpower'd
  Save he more clement prove.

Each post that leaves the village gate
  My message forth doth bear,
But still forgotten here I wait
  And wither and despair.

Sir Cavalier, my mother dear,
  Must come and visit you ;
That mother dear, Sir Cavalier,
  The face of God may view.

I 'll climb the wall which towereth there
  And to the winds I 'll cry ;
They 've built for me a tomb so fair
  Of steel and ivory.

My mother has of griefs a store,
  And I have got my own,
Full keen and sore I here deplore,
  But ne'er for mine I moan.

When in my grave three years I 've lain,
If thou wouldst pass thereby,
And but to breathe my name wouldst deign,
My dead bones would reply.

Sire nor mother me caress,
For I have none on earth,
One little brother I possess
And he 's a fool by birth.

If thou another man shouldst wed
And I the same should know,
In mourning clad from foot to head
For ever I would go.

Unless within a fortnight's space
Thy face, O maid, I see,
Flamenca, of Egyptian race,
My lady love shall be.

Flamenca of Egyptian race,
If thou wert only mine,
Within a bonny crystal case
For life I 'd thee inshrine.

Extend to me the hand so small,
Wherein I see thee weep,
For, oh thy palmy tear-drops all
I would collect and keep.

I wash'd not in the limpid flood
The goodly shirt, I fear ;
I wash'd it in the steaming blood
Of my betrothed fair.

Thou 'rt not, sweet dame, who smil'st so mild
  The mother me who bore,
She left me whilst a little child
  And fled and came no more.

Each morning when from bed I rise,
  'Tis then I lave my face
In tears, which from these wretched eyes
  Begin to flow apace.

Come to the window, sweet love, do,
  And I will whisper there
In Romany a word or two,
  And thee far off will bear.

Since from the town that lovely night
  We two together stray'd,
Your parents proud with wrath and spite
  Have war against me made.

A gypsy stripling's sparkling eye
  Has pierc'd my bosom's core,
A feat no eye beneath the sky
  Could e'er effect before.

Don't bid me from the land be gone
  And thou with child by me,
Each time I come the little one
  I 'd greet in Romany.

With such an ugly loathly wife
  The Lord has punished me,
I dare not take her for my life
  Where any one can see.

This night abroad the Gypsies stay,
  O mother thus we know a sign,
They 've to the shepherds ta'en their way
  To steal the lambkins fine.

Brown Egypt's race in days of old
  Were wont silk hose to wear,
But for their sins so manifold
  They now must fetters bear.

That spirit long opprest with grief
  Hath 'scap'd and heavenward flown,
In hopes the Lord will grant relief
  Who builds in heaven his throne.

May blessings shower upon thy head,
  Thou woman kind and fair,
Though thou hadst but one loaf of bread,
  With me thou that didst share.

I 've call'd thee thrice in anxious strain,
  But thou dost not appear,
And should I raise my voice again
  Thy kinsmen me would hear.

Above there in the dusky pass
  Was wrought a murder dread,
The murdered fell upon the grass,
  Away the murderer fled.

O never with the Gentiles wend,
  Nor ween their speeches true,
Or else be certain in the end
  Thy blood will lose its hue.

O never with the Gentiles wend,
  Nor in their vows delight,
Unless thou wish that in the end
  Thy blood like theirs be white.

The Lord He when . . .[1] as . . .[1] state
  With [E]gypt's race was bred,
And when he won to man's estate
  His blood the Gentiles shed.

[1] MS. illegible.

THE RIGHTEOUS MAN

THE man that 's righteous
By tyrants threaten'd
Rebelleth never,
Though full of woe ;
His righteousness
His safeguard is,
But their wickedness layeth
The wicked low.

THE SONG OF DEBORAH

For vengeance vouchsaf'd unto Israel,
When the people their lives with devotion
Did stake, ever bless'd be Jehovah !

Hark, hark, O ye kings and ye princes !
To Jehovah a song I 'm inditing,
A psalm to the High God of Israel.

When thou went'st forth from Seir, O Jehovah !
When thou strod'st from the grass-plain of
Edom,
The earth shook and trembled ; the heavens
Flung open their flood-gates ; the black clouds
In water did burst, whilst the mountains
Before the dread face of Jehovah
Did melt ; even Sinai melted
Before the Jehovah of Israel.

In the days of Shamgar Ben Anath,
In the days of Jael, the highways
Were abandon'd and travellers trembling
By bye-ways and crooked paths wended ;
The villages all were abandon'd—
And so matters continued in Israel
Till up rose I, Deborah, destin'd
To serve as a mother in Israel.

New gods for themselves they elected—
O then at the gates there was warfare !
But who saw a spear or a buckler
'Midst twice twenty thousand in Israel ?
My heart's with the bold ones of Israel,
Who stak'd with truest devotion
Their lives—ever bless'd be Jehovah !

O ye ! who now ride on white asses,
Ye who sit in the places of judgment,
Who travel the highways in safety,
Proclaim of Jehovah the mercies !—

And Jehovah's mercies proclaim'd they
In the places for drawing up water,
Undisturb'd by the whizzing of arrows ;
Jehovah's mercies proclaim'd they,
Vouchsaf'd to the hamlets of Israel.
Once more in the cool of the evening
To the gates God's people descended.

Wake, Deborah, wake and be singing
A song rousing heroes to battle !

Rise, son of Abinoam, Barak !
And lead thou captivity captive.

Then the people throng'd to their nobles,
The Lord made me captain in Israel.
From Ephraim e'en to Amalek
The roots of my people extended ;
'Midst my people I Benjamin reckon'd.

. . . . .

With me were the chiefs of Issachar ;
With Deborah also was Barak.
I sent them on foot to the valleys.

Amidst the divisions of Reuben
Are hearts fraught with deepest imaginings—
Then wherefore ever, O Reuben,
Art thou by thy sheepfolds reclining,
To the bleating of silly flocks listening ?—
Thy heart is sagacious, O Reuben !

. . . . .

Bold Zebulon, scoffing at danger,
Emperilled his life on the mountains
With Naphtali, equally gallant,
In the cause of the Lord God Jehovah.

The kings in their might came to battle,
The Canaanite kings came to Taanach ;
By the pools of Megiddo they fought us
But no booty of silver obtain'd they ;
From on high fought the stars against Sisera,
They fought from their courses against him ;
Brook Kison away bore the corses,
A fam'd, ancient stream is brook Kison.
Then trampled my soul on the mighty ;
Then the shoes of the horses were splinter'd
By spurnings, by desperate spurnings.
Accurs'd be the dwellers of Merog !
Cried the Angel high of Jehovah ;
To Jehovah's assistance they came not
In the fight 'gainst the godless and mighty !
But bless'd above women be Jael,
The brave wife of Heber the Kennite ;

When Sisera ask'd but for water
Rich cream she to Sisera handed,
Rich cream in the goblet of splendour ;
To the nail her left hand she extended,
With her right she held firmly the hammer,
On the nail down with force came the hammer,
And the tyrant was pierc'd through the temple ;
To her feet down bent him the tyrant,
To her feet down bent he and tumbled,
And lay where he tumbled, a carcass.
From the window looks forth, from the casement,
The mother of Sisera, and crieth :
'Why comes not my son ? why delays he ?
Why loiter the wheels of his chariot ? '
But soon to her own self respondeth
That woman so fam'd for her wisdom—
She answers herself in this fashion :
'But no doubt a great spoil they have gather'd,
And are busied their spoil in dividing ;
There 's a maid, perhaps two, for each warrior,
And spoil of all colours for Sisera,
Embroider'd work, dyed of all colours,
Needle-work for the neck of the spoiler.'
So crieth the mother of Sisera—
May Jehovah's foes perish like Sisera !
And may those who revere thee, Jehovah !
Shine bright, as the sun, when he rises.

THE MAGICIAN

Al-Sim was the name they gave
To the beast when it first saw day ;
The fell hyena was his sire,
His dam the she-wolf gray.

The wizard muttered a secret spell,
And he beckoned with his wand,
And at his summons Al-Sim came
Louping across the sand.

'Cross the desert sand of Palestine
From the graves of the dead he came,
From doing that which is his wont
On the life-deserted frame.

Around the circle thrice he ran
To the clouds he yell'd so high,
But at the shake of the wizard's wand
He cower'd and ceas'd his cry.

' Thee from the grave-feast I have call'd,
Yet must thou not complain,
For a costlier feast and savourier far
I 'm about for thee to gain.'

To a young man he 's changed
  Of fair and regal mien,
And has form'd for him a white turban
  All out of palm-leaves green.

And the pebble-stones on the sand that lay
  Have the guise of diamonds ta'en,
And they bedeck that fair turban
  As a glorious, glorious chain.

And the scimitar in its sheath of gold,
  That before Al-Sim hung,
Was formed from out a blasted bough,
  That above the wizard swung.

Then he whisper'd in Al-Sim's ear
  And his purpose let him know,
And a flush of wild joy thereupon
  Mantled the brute-man's brow.

A rout of wolves pursuing deer
  Was sweeping the wilds along,
And the wolves have chang'd to horsemen tall,
  And the deer to coursers strong.

And Al-Sim at that wild troop's head
  On a camel-leopard rode,
And they 're away by the break of day
  To the King's daughter's abode.

'The King that dwells on Lebanon
  He is my deadly foe,
And he has got a fair daughter,
  And to win her thou shalt go.'

THE PURSUIT OF WISDOM

O THOU who fain wouldst wisdom gain,
Strive night and day untir'd,
For by repeated toil and pain
It is alone acquir'd.

THE WARRIOR

THOU lov'st to look on myrtles green,
And the narcissus bright of hue ;
I love the blaze of sabres keen,
I love the dagger's flash to view.

Thou, thou may'st drink the rosy wine
From golden goblets sculptured o'er ;
From foemen's skulls the joy be mine
To drink my foemen's reeking gore.

THE RENEGADE

Now pay ye the heed that is fitting,
  Whilst I sing ye the Iran adventure ;
The pasha on sofa was sitting,
  'Midst his harem's glorious centre.

Greek sang, and Tcherkass, for his pleasure,
  And Kergoosian captive is dancing ;
In the eyes of the first heaven's azure,
  In the others black Eblis is glancing.

But the pasha's attention is failing,
  O'er his visage his fair turban stealeth ;
From chebouk he sleep is inhaling,
  Whilst around him sweet vapours he dealeth.

What rumour without is there breeding ?
  Ye fair ranks asunder why wend ye ?
Kyslar Aga, a strange captive leading,
  Cometh forward, and crieth ' Efendy.'

' Whose face has the power when present
  'Mong the stars round the divan which muster ?
Who amidst the gems of night's crescent
  Has the blaze of Aldeboran's lustre ?

‘ Glance nearer, bright star ! I have tiding,
Glad tiding. Behold how in duty
From far Lehistan the wind gliding
Has brought this fresh tribute of beauty.

‘ In the padishaw’s garden there bloometh
In proud Istambul no such blossom ;
From the wintry regions she cometh,
Whose memory so lives in thy bosom.’

Then the gauzes removes he which shade her,
At her beauty all wonder intensely ;
One moment the pasha surveyed her,
Then, dropping his chebouk, without sense lay.

His turban has fallen from his forehead,
To assist him the bystanders started ;
His mouth foams, his face blackens horrid,—
See, the Renegade’s soul has departed !

HYMN TO MAHOMET

O ENVOY of Allah, to thee be salaam,
With my whole heart I love thee, O blest be thy name.
At the high throne of God thou for sinners dost plead
Who forgives for thy sake each iniquitous deed.
O Prophet of Allah, for all that I 've done
Of rebellion against Him, 'tis thou must atone.
For thou art the one intercessor, thou, thou,—
The prince of the prophets to whom the rest bow.
In the world's Judgment Day when all nations are met,
When good deeds and bad in the balance are set,
Intercession I hope for, from thee, only thee,
So breathe intercession for me, wretched me.
'Tis true my misdeeds I 'm unable to count,
But I know that thy goodness exceeds their amount.
Like one who 's defunct I a long time have been,
My body is drowned in an ocean of sin.
My rebellions they be of so dreadful a dye
That to wend to my Maker no courage have I.
Now save I in dust at thy feet myself throw,
And thy footstool I strike with my agonis'd brow ;
And save thou for me dost benignantly speak,
What for me will remain but despairing to shriek ?

For unless I thy kind intercession procure,
My soul with the Kaffirs will torments endure.
But I trust thou wilt that for thy servant employ
And that rest I shall gain, and unspeakable joy.
Unto thee without end shall be praises and prayers,
And also to them, thy disciples and heirs,
The voyagers noble who trod the true road,
And to others the path of salvation who show'd,
The four eldest friends of exalted degree
Who of our religion the four pillars be.
First of all the good King of the Kingdom of Grace,
The just Abou Bekir with truth in his face;
The next the stout lion so bravely who warr'd,
The Lyon of the Mussulman, Omar my Lord.
The third a high Emir, renowned 'midst our clan,
The child of the moment, the Emir Othman.
The fourth of the pillars, my Lord Ali dear,
Inspector acute of the dark and the clear.
Then the light of our eyes, the delectable twain,
The lovely Prince Hassan, the Emir Hoseyn.
Nor unnoticed by men shall be suffered to pass
Those excellent uncles, Hamzah and Abbass.
Unto each of that band be a thousand salaams,
And bless'd through all ages be each of their names.

EPIGRAMS

I

HEAR what once the pigmy clever
To the stupid giant said :
Things are not of highest value
Which do highest rear their head ;
The sluggish horse is nothing better
Than the donkey lowest bred.

II

The man who of his words is sparing
His strength and weakness hidden keeps ;
Think not every thicket empty,
Perchance in one a tiger sleeps.

III

If thou wouldst ruin escape, and blackest woe,
Unto these words, these precious words attend :
Never be heedless of a mortal foe,
Nor choose a proud and envious man for friend.

IV

Sit down with your friends in delightful repose
When war and contention you see 'midst your foes ;
But when to an end their contentions they bring,
Then, then seize the bow, and get ready the sling.

V

The hungry hound upon the bone will pounce
  He prowling finds, and not mistrustful pass;
He asks not whom it did belong to once,
  The prophet's camel or the sinner's ass.

VI

Though God provides our daily bread,
  Yet all must seek that bread, I ween;
Though all must die, there is no need
  To rush the dragon's jaws between.

VII

If in the boor's garden the King eats a pear,
His servants rapacious the tree will uptear;
For every five eggs he gives bounteously, more
Than five hundred fowls will his armies devour.

VIII

If the half of a loaf the devout man receives,
The half of that half to the wretched he gives;
But no sooner a tyrant one kingdom has ta'en,
Than the wish of his heart is another to gain.

IX

If a cat could the power of flying enjoy,
She all the world's sparrows would quickly destroy;
If power in the hands of a beggar you place,
No mercy he 'll show to the beggarly race.

X

The tailor who travels in far foreign lands,
Can always get bread by the work of his hands ;
But the king who from throne and from country
has fled,
Must oft without supper go sighing to bed.

XI

Of the children of wisdom how like is the face
To pure gold that 's accepted in every place ;
But the ignorant great are much like leather cash,
At home which though current, abroad is but
trash.

XII

So much like a friend with your foe ever deal,
That you never need dread the least scratch from
his steel ;
But ne'er with your friend deal so much like a foe,
That you ever must dread from his faulchion a
blow.

HAFIZ'S DRINKING SONG

O Thou whose equal mind knows no vexation,
Who holding love in deep abomination,
On love's divan to loiter wilt not deign,
Thy wit doth merit every commendation.
Love's visions never will disturb the brain
Of him who drinks the noble wine's oblation ;
And know, thou passion-smit, pale-visag'd swain,
There 's medicine to work thy restoration—
In mind, O Hafiz, the receipt retain—
'Tis quaffing winecups to intoxication.

RICH AND POOR

WHERE income there 's not, the expense should be small—
A sailor thus sang from the mast head on high—
Should no showers of rain in the Kohistan fall,
The Tigris's bed in a year would be dry.

In his low and light tent the poor Gypsy doth sit,
The King in his palace so massive and tall,
But soon for the same quiet mansion must quit
The Gypsy his tent and the Monarch his hall.

Great Caroun is dead and forgotten ; the man
Who left forty castles replete with gold store,
But living, though dead, is the great Nourshivan,
In the good name he left he has death triumph'd o'er.

THE POWER OF BEAUTY

THE handsome of face in each spot is ador'd,
Though his father and mother be slain by the sword.
A peacock I saw on the blest Koran book,
Said I, ' Out of place on that volume you look.'
' Hold your tongue,' said the bird, ' none will lift up a hand
'Gainst one that is lovely, where'er he may stand.'
To the child with a countenance bright as the sun
What matters if father and mother are gone ?
He 's a jewel that never neglected will lie,
For a bright precious pearl every mortal will buy.

THE POWER OF VOICE

How sweetly the voice, as I lay half in dream,
Of a songster at daybreak upon my ear stole.
O better than beauty a sweet voice, I deem ;
One pleases the eye, but the other the soul.

PENITENCE

THY qualities, Lord, are so many and grand,
The courage soon cools which would them understand;
Thy attributes, Master, can no one report;
To know Thee, O Master, all knowledge is short.
The wisest becomes but a poor, simple elf,
Who'd know Thee. One knows Thee and that is Thyself.
O God, from the time of my birth I have been
A reprobate steep'd most deeply in sin,
A slave to each beauty my eyes did behold,
With the miseries of youth I untimely grew old;
My head void [of] brain was with wind soon replete,
And I rush'd like a moth my destruction to meet.
Athirst for the goblet, the lip of my love,
I hover'd and flutter'd the goblet above;
And as passion for wine with my lust I combined,
No wonder devotion soon went to the wind!
Ablution to make if a pitcher I took,
Methought that its water of wine had the look;
I dreamt of my God and His precepts no more,
All kind of devotion I quickly gave o'er.
But prayers would ne'er cleanse, though a hundred each day,
A heart that like mine was so distant away.

To the mosque if I go under colour of prayer,
It is but to gaze on some beauteous one there.
If my visage I turn to the holy one's shrine,
If my hands I in prayer like a suppliant join,
I think of some fair one that nigh to me stands,
It is in her worship I lift up my hands.
If my soul I can't make to conform to Thy laws,
O God, make its sin to rescue it a cause.
O God, Thou art rich and all power dost claim,
Rebellion and homage to Thee are the same.
Should the world for a thousand years homage to Thee pay,
The world could not add to Thy glory a ray;
Should the world for a thousand years homage refuse,
No ray of Thy glory, O Lord, Thou wouldst lose.
O Lord, disobedient I 've hitherto been,
But let me no longer continue in sin.
If I have not centr'd in Thee my desires,
If I have [not] done what Thy justice requires,
Point out to me kindly the only true road,
And make Thou it easy and soft to be trod.
With the light of Thy visage my eye render clear,
Make my heart with Thy knowledge a rose garden fair,
Let my soul not go erring in darkness of night,
Illumine its path from the fountain of light,
Exterior love far from my bosom remove,
Its recesses fill all with the light of Thy love;
Let my glances ne'er miss Thee, wherever they flit,
Let Thy name be the word on my heart that is writ.

So fill with Thy love, O most mighty, my breast,
So lighten that cell long with darkness distrest,
That the secret of secrets to me being known,
I my Maker may view in each thing I look on.
In each thing whereon gazes the waken'd up soul
God's face be apparent, unclouded and whole;
Of the cup of Thy love my heart drink deep,
That it out of death to existence may leap,
And that drunk with the love of my Lord ever I
No object in Nature save Him may descry;
That my heart wean'd from earth and the things of the clod
May testify ever of God, only God.
Else cause such destruction my soul to come o'er,
That no portion or vestige remain of it more.
My spirit with truth render prudent and old,
My heart with religion adorn as with gold;
Make verity ever the garment I wear,
Make thanks for Thy goodness the coinage I bear.
Keep my heart free from all that 's to falsehood allied,
My breast free from passion, from malice and pride.
On my qualities working, Lord, alter them all,
Now for other great mercies on Thee I will call;
Of my passion satanic extinguish the fire,
But awaken my love and my pious desire.
Suffer not in my soul concupiscence to storm,
To the dictates of chastity make it conform.
Consume me not, Lord, with Thy terrible ire,
With the water of clemency temper its fire.
I say not in darkness give error to me,
But let all my actions with justice agree;

As a guide in the way divine confidence lend,
Till I reach the Caaba to which my hopes tend.
Be content the provision I use on the road,
Till I reach the pavilion and presence of God.
When Thou with religion my soul dost array,
In all things the law may I strictly obey ;
Let worship to Thee be a custom in me,
But let not such custom my worship e'er be.
In every kyam make my body erect,
And upright my worship in every respect,
In every rakoua my stature bend low,
Till the centre of bliss in that posture I know.
My thoughts in this worship put all when [I] pray,
To no other object permit them to stray.
Let me rise with fresh vigour from every kaoud,
Be the ground of my confidence stable and good.
My devotion do Thou from hypocrisy clear
And with Thy sincerity make me sincere.
My obedience increase to Thy law till I be
Entitled to rank with the hallow'd sunnee.

THE WAY OF NATURE

THE tree that is bitter by birth and race
If in Paradise garden to grow you place,
And water it free with the streams' brine
That yield in Paradise nectar and wine,
At the end its quality still declares,
For bitter is all the fruit it bears.

Should you feed the bird upon its nest
With figs immortal, food of the blest,
And give to drink from Silsibal,
Whilst life in the egg breathes Gabriel,
A raven, a raven the egg shall bear
And the peacock shall mourn its care.

FERIDUN

No face of an angel could Feridun claim,
Nor of musk nor of amber, I ween, was his frame;
In bright generosity beauteous was he,
Be generous like him and as fair thou shalt be.

ZULEKA

Thus says this rhetorician, this measurer of words,
Who in his magazine has a treasure of words
That in the kingdom of Africa there lived a king in glory, a king whose name was Timaus ;
All the attributes of royalty did he possess.
There did not remain a wish ungratified in his heart ;
His crown derived lustre from his brow,
His throne received elevation from his foot ;
Fortune made a girth for his horse out of the sign of the Twins ;
Victory was strongly bound to the chain of his sword ;
He had a beautiful daughter, by name Zuleka,
Who of all the world had the superiority ;
No starry daughter of the castle of Kings,
No glittering pearl out of the royal degree,
Does not mingle in the description of her beauty.
I will endeavour to describe her exterior,
From head to foot I will go down ; like her hair
I am glittering in my thought from the reflection of her face,
From her sweet ruby I cry for assistance,
In her description what I know I will again repeat ;
Her figure, a palm tree, created out of mercy ;

From the garden of grace her head arises,
From the imperial river water drinking,
From the head of the fountain water bearing,
In the separation of her hair is the snare of wise
men ;
From it and musk a separation not considerable,
Her abundant hair the comb which separates,
Which makes a delicate separation in the midst
of it,
From the separation of the two parts has the soul
of a musk phial,
And out of them comes musk as from a scent
bottle,
Down weighed the tresses smelling like jasmines,
The bough of the rose casts a shade on her foot,
Her two tresses two black ropes,
From the beech tree of her lofty head rope dancers,
Heaven the school of her beauty taught,
Placed out of her brow a silver board.
On the side of the silver board she show'd
Two n's (brows) below her head, anointed with
musk,
Below these two n's pleasant two sads, eyes
Wrote the pen of the work master
From the confine of these n's to the circle of the
m (mouth).
After the fashion of an alif arose a nose of silver,
Increased under the alif the cypher of the mouth,
One after ten made the troubles of the world.
Her s's (teeth) clear out of rubies laughing,
Of the open mouth the tus in the teeth.
Her face a model of the garden of Aram,
In it opened roses of various colours.

THE MANDCHOU DESERT

Hail to the Mandchou desert.
  From out thee came the bands
Who won the plains of China
  By dint of valiant hands.

EPIGRAMS

I

THERE 's no living, my boy, without plenty of gold,
But gold to obtain you must ever be bold.
The Diver will never who feareth the shark
Bring up precious pearls from the sea caverns dark.

II

O think not you 'll change what on high is designed,
Though you lift up your hands and to heaven you shout ;
The angel will grieve not, who governs the wind,
Though a gust should the lamp of the widow blow out.

III

Load not thyself with gold, O mortal man, for know
No strength thou 'lt have for loads when summon'd hence away.
Avoid excess of meat, it maketh gross, I trow,
And gross thou must not be when summon'd hence away ;
For through the narrow gate thou 'lt find it hard to go
Of death, if thou art gross when summon'd hence away.

EPIGRAMS

I

Assume a friend's face when a foeman you spy,
For his hatred you 'll turn into friendship thereby,
Deal gentle words round you when threats are
outpoured,
For not against silk do we use the sharp sword.
By means of caresses and promises fair,
The elephant fierce you may guide with a hair.

II

The lion in woods finds prey of noble kind,
In fields of air the hawk sufficient meat;
He who would hunt within a house confined,
Must needs possess the spider's hands and feet.

III

To trust a man I never feel inclined,
Unless I know his very inmost mind;
Better an open foe your flesh should rend,
Than you should deem a secret foe your friend.

IV

A hunter who was always seeking game
In evil hour upon a tiger came;
Chance to the hunter is not always kind,
Instead of game he may a tiger find.

V

The plans of men of shrewdest wit
  To fail are known,
Whilst beardless lads the mark will hit
  By chance alone.

VI

Well was it said, long years ago,
Never trust him whom you 've given a blow ;
Trust not the heart you have caused to ache,
For thine, if it can, it will surely break.
Fling not a stone at the wall of a town,
Lest one from the rampart should strike you down.

VII

Who roams the world by many wants beset,
Is quickly glad his own name to forget ;
Unless you 've gold you cannot do much harm,
And if you 've gold you need no other arm.
Gold if you lack you cannot cross the brine ;
Better than ten men's strength is one man's coin.

EPIGRAMS

I

A WORTHLESS thing is song, I trow,
From out the heart which does not flow ;
But song from out no heart will flow
Which does not feel of love the glow.

II

Though pedants have essayed to hammer
Into our heads the points of grammar ;
We 're oft obliged to set at nought
The different force of *should* and *ought* ;
And oft are sorely puzzled whether
We should make use of *both* or *either*.

III

When of yourself you have cause to speak
Always make yourself broad and tall ;
Envy attacks you if you are great,
But thorough contempt attends the small.

EPIGRAMS

HONESTY

No wonder honesty 's a lasting article,
Seeing that people seldom use a particle.

A POLITICIAN

He served his God in such a fashion
As ne'er put Satan in a passion.

THE CANDLE

For foolish pastimes oft, full oft, they thee ignite,
I oft a pastime prove for tongues with folly rife ;
By wasting of thyself thou yieldest others light,
And I in selfsame way must use my luckless life.

THE THREE EXPECTANTS

There are three for my death that now pine,
  Though one and all wondrous civil;
Would that all of them hung on a line,
  My children, the worms, and the Devil.

My body, my soul, and my gear,
  When down to the grave I descend,
The three hope among them to share,
  And to revel on time without end.

But there is not one of the three,
  To the others though kindly affected,
For both of their shares would agree
  To resign his own portion expected.

The Devil, so harsh and austere,
  Who only in evil hath joy,
Would scorn to take body and gear
  For my soul, that sweet beautiful toy.

My children would rather possess
  The gear I have toil'd so to gather,
Though for me fervent love they profess,
  Than the body and soul of their father.

The worms, though my children will make
  A lament when I 'm laid in the hole,
Would my body in preference take
  To my gear or my beautiful soul.

Oh, Christ! who wast hung on a tree,
  And wast pierc'd by a fool in his madness;
Since each of them plund'ring would be,
  Send each disappointment and sadness.

A HYMN

O Jesus, Thou Fountain of solace and gladness
  Of Heaven's high Three second person divine;
Forgive, O forgive me my blindness and madness,
  And guide to Thy kingdom this spirit of mine.

Dearly, O Jesus,
  Thou boughtest me,
Yon Friday dark
  Upon the tree.

Thy foes were numerous,
  Fierce and fell;
Few and weak those
  Who wished Thee well.

Nigh stood Thy mother,
  Full of fears,
Wringing her hands
  And bathed in tears.

Often, O Jesus,
  Wilfully
With my great sins
  I 've tortured Thee.

Causing Thy wounds
  To open again,
Waking anew
  The ancient pain.

All the kindness
  Thou hast display'd,
With black ingratitude
  I 've repaid.

But Jesus, Creator of earth and of ocean,
  Who me, a vile sinner, so dearly didst buy ;
My damnable ignorance turn to devotion,
  And guide my poor soul to Thy courts in the
      sky.

SAINT JACOB

SAINT JACOB he takes our blest Lord by the hand:
'I gladly would Christianize Garsia land.'

'O how wilt thou bring it within Christian pale?
No ship hast thou here o'er the salt sea to sail.'

'Thy power, O Lord, is so wondrously great,
Full quickly a ship Thou for me canst create.'

'Saint Jacob, hie down to the salt ocean strand,
There standeth so little a stone by the land.'

Saint Jacob he taketh a book in his hand,
And down he proceeds to the salt ocean strand.

Saint Jacob he made o'er the stone the cross-mark,
From the land straight it floated, as though 'twere a bark.

It rode o'er the billows so rapid and free,
Right, right towards Garsia promontoree.

So rapid the stone to glide thither began,
A hundred miles space in one short hour it ran.

In comes a foot-boy, to the King doffs his bonnet:
'Here cometh a stone, and a man sits upon it.'

A woman rushed in, in her eyes wonder shone :
' Here cometh a man, and he sits on a stone.'

King Garsia taketh his axe in his hand,
And down he proceeds to the salt ocean strand.

' Now hear thou, Saint Jacob, I say unto thee,
What hast thou in this land, in this land here with me ? '

' Unto thee I am come to this land 'cross the brine,
Because that my Maker is greater than thine.'

' O how can thy Maker be greater than mine ?
Mine drinks every day the brown mead and the wine.'

' O then my Creator is greater than thine,
For mine can the water convert into wine.

' My Maker can turn the black mould into bread,
Can give life back to them who long, long have been dead.'

' If thou canst restore me my dearly loved son,
I 'll trust in thy Maker, and no other one.

' If I again view him, with flesh and hair dight,
As he fifteen years since disappeared from my sight ;

' If I get him again both with hawk and with hound,
Just, just as he sank in the depths of the sound ;

'With hair on his head, and with flesh on his bone,
As though he the pang of death never had known.'

Then the blessed Saint Jacob upon his book pored:
''Twill be no easy matter to get him restored.'

When he had stood reading a wee little time,
He raised up the man from hell's sorrowful clime.

'Now again thou hast got him with flesh and hair dight,
As he fifteen years since disappeared from thy sight.

'Thou hast got him again, both with hawk and with hound,
Just, just as he sank in the ocean profound.

'With hair on his head, and with flesh on his bone,
As though he the pang of death never had known.'

'Now hear thou, my dear son, so fine and so fair,
What news from thy journey afar dost thou bear?'

'The news which I bring from the far distant place,
Is that one little knows of the other's hard case.

'There the woman, who 's hated the child of her womb,
Out of the snake-tower can ne'er hope to come.

'There the cruel step-mother, her child who has slain,
Goes begirt with a sword fraught with festering bane.

'The merchants who here in heaps money uprake,
There hiss in the likeness of serpent and snake.

'The Sysselmen, wretches with hearts hard as stone,
There in the snake-tower despairingly moan.'

SONG

I 'VE pleasure not a little
  A dancing youth to see,
Nor less—one single tittle—
  An old man full of glee.

To dance I ever glory
  With those of youthful mien ;
It shows, although I 'm hoary
  In hair, my mind is green.

THE BARD AND THE DREAMS

O'ER the sweet-smelling meads with his lyre in
his hand
The bard was straying;
In the twilight of evening, refreshing and bland,
His chords were playing.
He sang of the flowrets that slept in the tomb,
He sang of the flowrets that poured their perfume,
He sang of the flowrets that yet were to bloom.

And the rose departed,
A smile from its sepulchre darted;
And the rose yet living with blushes of red
Breathed sweets o'er his head.
And the rose which unborn concealed yet lies,
Seemed to open before his eyes.
By a fountain's side with verdure array'd
Himself he laid.

And the murmur and hum of the pure water
fleeting,
And the strains, which the birds of the wood were
repeating,
And the innocent heart, which so peaceful was
beating,
Shed health-giving slumbers,
On lids which no sorrow cumbers.

In the visions of sleep there came to his side
  A sire with locks snow-hoary;
And the songster sped with that sire for his guide
  To an unknown territory.

On ruins majestic himself he found,
The mouldering bones of old heroes lay round;
  Their ghosts awaking
  Rose from their graves wild gestures making.
  The youth was quaking—
But the old man smiled as his mind he led
To the kempion times long fled.

Then a lamp in the night's deep silence shone
  Through the dingy mould,
And under the masses of fallen stone
  There glittered gold.

To the harp then pointing the sage disappears,
And the youth shed tears.
'Yes, yes, the young bard thy countenance
    knows,'
  So sang in wild passion the boy—
'Not in vain in my bosom a holy fire glows,
Not in vain thy bright lamp the grave's mystery
    shews,
  The bard will obey thee with joy.'

Again there appeared in the dreams of the
    stripling
  A being who held him intent;
It came as in flood come the high billows rippling,
  Like billows when ebbing it went.

Though the look of an aged and slow female
wearing,
It ran like the breezes in spring time careering,
Full often it vanished with threatening bearing.
But suddenly caught he the fugitive wild,
And then by his breast a maiden smil'd.
'Thee often I 've met on life's journey,' he said,
'And when like a meteor thou past me hast sped,
I 've seen thee look backward—and threaten.

'O! kiss me, sweet maiden, ere on thou dost stray,
I 've seen thee with flowers strew the wanderer's
way.
They lived in their brightness,
When thou in this lightness,
Had'st fled farthest off; and sometimes they
became.
A Bauta-stone over the worm-wasted frame.

'Vouchsafe me a smile,' said the youth, 'I entreat,
I know thy course lightning-fleet.
Thy light pinions ever
Thou pliest, sweet giver
Of palms, verdant palms, to the stripling so
clever,
Who caught thee, though lightning fleet.'

Again to his eye a fair vision was given,
A being angelical stood in the heaven.
In morn's fresh rose-hues drest
Stood the spirit blest.
As shines from above
The starlet of love,

So kindled his glance toward earth's gentle child.
  As the maid to her beckons the youth she loves dearly,
  When vespers are chiming and Luna shines clearly,
So toward him beckoned the Angel, and smil'd.

With rapture the songster took thither his way,
Where the winged one of heaven stood beauteous and gay.
But, just as he hoped that the height was surmounted,
Far distant again they each other confronted.
And still the Angel beckoned there,
But—never, never near.
'My seraph! wilt ever avoid my embrace?'
—Said the youngster with mortified mien—
'But though I'm unable to climb to thy place,
My eye thou hast blest from the mansions of grace,
  And thy heaven, thou distant, I've seen.'

His slumber departed, his visions they fled,
But oft when he harped they came into his head.
'Blest, trebly blest, may our life be regarded,
For unto me here threefold life is awarded.

'See the roselet departed,
A smile from its tomb has darted.
  And the rose, which yet lives in blushes and bloom,
  Breathes o'er me perfume.
Yes, from its concealment, the unborn rose
Before me seems to unclose.'

LINES

To read the great mysterious past
  They are yearning;
But to mist, the writings old fast, fast
  Are turning.

O, how inviting
  The deeds of yore!
But the ancient writing
  Mist sweeps o'er.

THE WISE WELOND

WHERE are now the bones
Of the wise Welond,
The gold smith
Who was most unfortunate,
I say of
The wise Welond,
Because one may not to any
Of the dwellers of the earth
Destroy the craft
Which Christ has lent him,
Nor may one
More easily
Any unfortunate
Deprive of his craft
Than one might undertake
To turn the sun back,
Or any man
This swift firmament
From its right course.
Who knows now
In what grave heap
Rocks cover
The bones of the wise
Welond?

THE FAIRIES' SONG

BALMY the evening air,
  Nature, how bright the hue!
But, though the bloom is fair
  The sense with sweets to woo,
Love, Music, Mirth, Oh give!
  On these we fairies live!

The glow-worm's amorous lamp
  Recalls her wandering mate;
Their revel in the swamp
  Outshines the halls of State.
Then, Spirits, hither fly,
  And match their revelry!

The Bat is on the wing,
  And Gnats, what reels they run!
In wide or narrow ring,
  An atmosphere of fun.
Then let us to the dance,
  And feet like midges glance!

AN ELEGY

WHERE shall I rest my hapless head,
  Heavy with grief? how plenteously
Must I the briny torrents shed—
  Alack, and woe is me!

Our chief is gone, at last, at last,
  The safeguard of our nation he;
The glory of our age is past—
  Alack, and woe is me!

Unto the swords, O father dear,
  Of foemen thirsting horribly
For blood, why leave thy children here?
  Alack, and woe is me!

Of justice is the fountain dried,
  And mute the law's high symphony;
Fallen is Europa's brightest pride—
  Alack, and woe is me!

There is a change of times and things
  That passeth on eternally,
Decreed by Him, the King of Kings—
  'Tis right—but woe is me!

Now is the earth with violets gay,
  And flowers manifold to see ;
Now frozen 'neath the winter's sway—
  How brief the roses be !

Now shews the sun his head of gold
  With a superior brilliancy ;
Now hides as were he dead and cold—
  Alack, and woe is me.

O father ! I will lave thy tomb
  With tear-drops well becoming me ;
Thy tomb with flowery herbs perfume—
  How brief the roses be !

LINES

How deadly the blow I received
When of thee, O my darling, bereaved !
No more up the hill I shall bound,
No strength in my poor foot is found ;
No joy o'er my visage shall break
Till from out the cold earth I awake.
Of the corn like the very top grain,
Or the pine 'mongst the shrubs of the plain,
Or the moon 'mongst the starlets above,
Wert thou amongst women, my love !

TO THE GIRL THEANOE

THY black and lustrous eyes, O Theanoe,
Like a wild consuming flame they make me go ;
They my senses take away,
And they burn me and they turn me into ashes with their ray,
O my beauteous Theanoe.

Thy lips, thy rosy lips, O Theanoe,
They hurl me to a hell of deepest woe ;
Thy mellow voice divine
With fire and desire doth fill this heart of mine,
O my beauteous Theanoe.

When first I did behold thee, Theanoe,
I felt of blessed hope a rushing flow,
Thou didst tell me then to love,
Now I shrivel and drivel, if from me thou dost but move,
O my beauteous Theanoe.

Thou didst kiss me in the mouth, O Theanoe,
And still upon my mouth remains a glow,
A kiss from thee had I,
Each swearing and declaring, we 'd together live and die,
O my gentle Theanoe.

THE WRESTLING-MATCH

As one day I wandered lonely, in extreme distress
of mind,
I a pleasant garden entered, hoping comfort there
to find.
Up and down I paced the garden till an open
space I spied,
There I saw a crowd of people, and I heard a voice
that cried :
'Come and see what Love is doing, here is Love
performing more
Wondrous feats than e'er were witnessed at
Olympian games of yore :
This he conquers, that he conquers, young and
old before him lie,
Great and small alike he conquers, none with him
a fall must try.'

Hearing this, at once I entered 'midst the crowd
collected there,
Some of whom no doubt were eager, like myself,
to banish care.
I would fain behold this being, this same wondrous
lad survey,
Who, 'twas said, in each encounter bore with ease
the prize away.

Quickly I the crowd divided, soon I pierced the multitude,
And this Love stood full before me, and what think you 'twas I view'd ?
Why, a boy, a little darling, full of captivating grace,
Rather roguish were his glances, but how lovely was his face !

Soon as I beheld this warrior, gibings I began to throw
At the wretches who had suffered fell defeat from such a foe.
Then, to me his visage turning, of the conquered standing by
One replied, and in replying tears he shed abundantly :
' O, poor youth,' 'twas thus he answered, ' little, little dost thou know
That in coming here thou comest not to joy, but bitter woe.
Tears and pains, and wounds most ghastly, wounds for which there is no cure,
Every kind of evil treatment such as no one can endure.'

When these words I heard him utter I was filled with bitter rage,
And forthwith made preparation with the warrior to engage.
' Hearken, Master Love,' I shouted, ' from this spot stir not away,
You and I must have a battle, must engage in deadly fray ;

That it may be known for certain which is
strongest of us two.'
Then into the arena bounding, there I stood in
all men's view,
In the midst of it expecting firm the onset of the foe,
Doubting not, should he attack me, him at once
to overthrow.
Love he was not slow to follow with a blythe and
joyous air,
Crying out, 'My dearest fellow, for the fight
yourself prepare!
Round the waist each other clasping, now let's
strive like wrestlers true,
Do your best and I will show you what young
Master Love can do.'

Then around the waist I clasped him, he his arms
around me wound,
Long we hugged and hugged each other, each his
match in t'other found.
Said at length the urchin to me: 'Sadly tired,
friend, am I,
Very much fatigued and weary, really, friend, just
fit to die.
Therefore take from me, I prythee, what thou
anxiously hast sought,
And for which in this arena with me gallantly
hast fought.'

Then a blast of wild consuming fire he breathed
into my breast,
Straight my breast it quick enkindled, all de-
prived was I of rest,

Then he ran away exulting to some other wretched
wight,
Such a zest he has for conflict, in such fray is his
delight.

As for me I fell half senseless on the fatal, fatal
spot,
Fierce consuming fire within me, never sure was
one so hot.
Rising up, I followed shrieking, 'Oh, have mercy,
Love, on me!
See my tears, my sad affliction, cure me of my
misery!'

Then he cried, 'Dost not remember all the boasts
thy lips out-pour'd?
Know henceforth in every region Love is Con-
queror and Lord.'

Thus he cried, and proudly left me, and wherever
now I rove,
I reproach myself for thinking I could vanquish
mighty Love.

TO THE SWALLOW

Thou art a constant comer
To us, O swallow dear,
In days of genial summer
To build and nestle here ;
But soon as summer 's ended,
Back, back to distant Nile,
By thee the way is wended,
Or Memphis' ruin'd pile.

Far more usurping passion
Doth seize upon my heart,
His dwelling there doth fashion
From whence he will not start ;
This love about is flying,
This is an eaglet still,
And this to thrust is trying
From out the shell his bill.

O what tiresome chirpings ever
From yonder brood ascend !
The greater loves endeavour
The younger ones to tend.
These younger, nourish'd quickly,
Do others procreate ;
The loves they swarm so thickly
I can't their numbers state.

ELEGY

How restless my slumber to-night ;
I have life but no longer delight :
All wither'd the heart in my breast,
With sorrow I 'm sadly opprest,
For cold in the grave-hill is laid
My dearly-lov'd beautiful maid ;
Her teeth were in whiteness like chalk,
Like harp-music the sound of her talk.
O fair as the foam of the tide,
Like the swan as it swims in its pride,
O pure as the new-fallen snow.
Thou left'st me behind thee in woe !
Of the vine O thou branch fresh and green,
O maiden of soft tender mien,
Thy cheek, of sweet smiles the abode,
A blush like the tender rose show'd !
O thou of the fingers so small,
Of the fair rounded bosom withal.

FAREWELL TO A FOUNTAIN WHERE HE PASSED ALL HIS EVENINGS

Farewell, O crystal fount ! away I ride—
Full time enough my tear-drops thou hast known
Mix with thy waters, and my ceaseless moan
Lament in vain a lovely ingrate's pride.

Farewell ; let it be bruited far and wide,
That I disturb thy quiet calm and lone
With accents lost when to her ears they 're blown,
As in the mighty sea is lost thy tide.

May toad nor viper with their noxious spume
Pollute thee ne'er, nor the tempest's roar
Disturb, till thou hast reach'd the ocean's womb,

And may the heart of her whom I adore
Ne'er thy flat inconstancy assume,
But the pure nature of thy crystal store.

THE DEAD MISTRESS

THE day my Lady into Heaven did glide,
The chosen Angels and the spirits blest
Around the new companion quickly press'd,
And her with wonder and compassion ey'd.

'What light is this? what beauty new?' they cried.
'No soul we 've seen in saintly charms so dress'd
Arrive from earth to this celestial rest
In all this age nor long preceding tide.'

She no wise sad herself at home to find,
With the most perfect mingled free and gay,
But often stops and partly looks behind

To see if I don't tread the upward way.
So I to heaven turn all my will and mind,
For that I 'd come in haste I hear her pray.

LAMENT

Sinnuccio mine, thou dolorous and lone,
By thee I 'm left, yet comfort still have I ;
Soon from the frame where thou didst prisoner lie
On wings of triumph thou hast upward flown,

Both poles thou seest from where thou now dost
wo[ne],
The wandering stars and how they zig-zag fly
And seest how circumscribed is human eye.
So in thy bliss all grievous thoughts I drown,

But I do beg thee in the realms of grace
Thou 'lt Guiton good and Master Dante greet,
Francesca too, and all that noble race,

And tell my Lady, when thou her dost meet,
That I grow almost mad when I retrace
Her holy actions and her visage sweet.

PASSION'S SLAVE

When for no victory yearneth
The soul, but glad and willing
  Becometh passion's slave,
To bane the counsel turneth
From friendship's lip distilling,
  And poisons whom 't would save.
That soul no victory earneth,
Which ne'er for victory yearneth,
  A willing, willing slave.

THE TYRANNY OF LOVE

THE fire Love enkindles
With bliss first warms our heart,
But soon, ah soon, the traitor
Doth burning pain impart.
Love's flame at first discloses
Pure innocence alone.
Alas ! can it the same be
Whereby foul guilt is shewn ?
O Love, thy bliss is vanish'd,
For in my Bride but falsehood
Now meets, alas, my sight.
Thy flame extinguish quite.

True Bliss, by virtue only known,
By virtue's self deserv'd alone,
For thee, and only thee, I sigh.
My sad heart would a heaven disdain,
Which through Dishonour it must gain.
So dear let slaves enjoyment buy.

The Soul can ne'er victorious prove,
Which to thy thrall, O tyrant Love,
Yields unresistingly.

LAMENT

THE columns broke the laurel green in twain,
My thoughts which shaded in the weary hour,
And I have lost what I shall find no more
From North to South, from Ind to Mauritayn.

By Death away my double treasure 's ta'en,
Which made me live with joy and walk with power,
What oriental gems can ne'er restore,
Nor force of gold or earth nor wide domain.

But since fate doth such mishap cause,
What can I do but have in heart despair,
Have eye-balls burn'd and a face down-bent ?

O life, in prospect thou who art so fair,
How easily in one brief morn is spent
What to acquire doth take an age of care !

A DRINKING SONG

O how my breast is glowing
  When I am drinking wine ;
And how my verse is flowing
  In honour of the nine.

How vanish grief and sorrow
  When I am drinking wine ;
Each thought about the morrow,
  Each project and design.

Through roseate space I 'm gliding
  When I am drinking wine ;
My spirit 'neath the guiding
  Of Bacchus, the divine.

I crown my head with flowers
  When I am drinking wine,
And say : ' Almighty powers,
  A quiet life be mine ! '

The air with sweets perfuming,
  When I am drinking wine,
I sit with damsel blooming
  Beneath a spreading vine.

No thought am I concealing
  When I am drinking wine ;
My bosom 's all revealing,
  I sit beneath the vine.

My tongue I watch not over
  When I am drinking wine ;
My heart I all discover,
  And naught within confine.

THE FALL OF THE ANGELS

THEN were plac'd in heaven
  At the Almighty's word
Glorious sons of splendour
  For to watch and ward.

And they watch'd and warded
  In the heavenly plains,
And they prais'd their Maker,
  Bright illustrious thanes.

O they were so happy,
  They knew nought of wrong,
Happy with their Monarch
  Liv'd they, O, how long.

Till at last discarding
  Their own reason's light,
They fell into error,
  Turn'd from what was right.

Whence arose such folly ?
  Why from over-pride;
They with their Creator
  Would the realm divide.

Them a leader chose they,
   Who his flag unfurl'd,
And would from Jehovah
   Wrest the Northern wor[l]d.

But Jehovah rous'd Him,
   Dreadful was His ire ;
And the rebels worsting,
   Hurl'd them into fire.

TO THE CREATOR

O God, the Creator of man and of Djinn,
Of the clear and the dark, of the outside and in,
I 'm nobler and better than all things that be,
In beauty and nature made perfect by Thee.
When my face Thou didst form, Thou that face
didst design,
As a glass to reflect the effulgence divine,
Wherein of perfection the Sun may be seen
Of beauty and grandeur of goodness, I ween.
O Thou, who adorn'd with all beauty dost gleam,
Who know'st all I do and my thoughts when I
dream,
For what were our beauty, unless it were meant
The beauty of God like a glass to present ?
What power in a handful of dust could be found,
Should make it a sun the whole world to astound ?
'Twas God the fair visage adorn'd with a light,
Which the garner of love e'en like straw did
ignite ;
'Twas God the lov'd visage so bland who did
make ;
'Twas God the lov'd visage so grand who did
make ;
'Twas God who bade twine the dark locks of
Mignon,
And a love-snare so fine did implant in each one.

When with loveliness perfect, O Lord, Thou mad'st man,
To display Thy own beauty, O Lord, was Thy plan.
And when on his beauty Thou look'st from above,
Upon Thy own beauty Thou lookest with love ;
And well with Thy beauty in love Thou may'st be,
For sure Thy own self is well worthy of Thee.

THE WARRIOR EARL

FELLER of the flying,
  Fain his Gods he 'd pray,
He the hauberk-wearer
  Heard a cheer for fray,
And high Hildur's herald
  Huge a raven saw.
Glad the faulchion-grasper
  Gothman's gore would draw.

Then 'gan the Earl the gallant
  Game of glaives to play,
Where before no warrior
  Won 'neath Sorva's sky ;
Ne'er bore foeman farther
  Fair gilt shield before,
Right the grim Earl goes through
  Gothland from the shore.

THE FAILURE

He who cast in simple mould
  Still and mute shall stand,
Though he live till grey and old
  Ne'er will wealth command.

LINES TO JOHN

There 's a dagger at your belt, John,
  A knife would suit it better ;
Ye have highland robes about ye,
  But ropes of straw were fitter ;
Ye have buckles on your shoes, John,
  Ye should have thongs of leather.

THE FLEA

A King in story noted
  A monstrous flea did own,
And on that flea he doted,
  As were it his own dear son ;
He calls a man of talent,
  A tailor he by trade ;
' Take measure of the gallant,
  For him let clothes be made.'

In silk and satin going
  Behold now good Sir Flea,
Ribbons are on him flowing
  And a golden cross has he ;
Now calls he his relations,
  He 's now Prime Minister,
To fill important stations
  And make at court a stir.

And soon the court half mad is,
  The fleas so sting and bite,
The Queen and waiting-ladies
  Can rest nor day nor night,
And dare not off to brush them,
  Far less the brutes to crack.
We happier far can crush them,
  When we catch them on our back !

THE WANDERING CHILDREN AND THE BENEVOLENT GENTLEMAN

AN IDYLL OF THE ROADS

ELDEST CHILD

O GENTLEMAN, sweet gentleman !
  To thee we humbly bow :
Upon poor hungry children three
  Your charity bestow !

We 've trudg'd the roads from rise of sun
  Until the sun is low,
And had no breakfast but the haws
  Which on the hedges grow.

BENEVOLENT GENTLEMAN

Poor vagrant children, I perceive
  You 've run away from home ;
But know that from such wickedness
  No good can ever come.

A cruel and a wicked thing
  It is, you must confess,
To run away from home and leave
  Your friends in deep distress.

O think upon your father's groans,
  Your mother's scalding tears,
Your sister's cries and agonies
  And your poor granny's fears.

ELDEST CHILD

Sweet gentle sir, your words are good,
We hear them thankfully;
But pray bestow with your advice
One single halfpenny!

BENEVOLENT GENTLEMAN

Return, poor thoughtless children, home,
Or evil will ensue.
There 's sad temptation in the world
For children such as you.

ELDEST CHILD

Oh clap a stopper to your jaw!
We hate such stuff and cant;
And keep your counsel for yourself,
The rhino 's what we want.

BENEVOLENT GENTLEMAN

Return to your paternal home,
Where peace you once enjoy'd;
Your morals, should you roam about,
Will quickly be destroy'd.

O it would be a dreadful thing,
A thing to break the heart,
If all your childish innocence
For ever should depart.

ELDEST CHILD

Get home, get home, you bloody old thief,
And do not chaff us so;
The pudding smokes—go home and stuff,
You bloody old parson, go!

BENEVOLENT GENTLEMAN

Farewell, poor babes ! go home to friends ;
They 'll open wide their arms ;
And you will rest beneath their roof
Disturb'd by no alarms.

ELDEST CHILD

Well, we have tramp'd the roads and queer'd
Full many a sharp and flat,
But ne'er by goles have we beheld
So cool a cove as that.

THE ELF BRIDE

There was a youthful swain one day
Did ted the new-mown grass ;
There came a gay and lovely may
From out the nigh morass.
Clad in a dress of silk was she,
Green as the leaves which deck the tree,
Her head so winsomely to see
With bulrush plaited was.

That lass he wooed, his suit she heeds,
And married are the pair ;
To bridal bed his wife he leads—
But what befell him there ?
He found, fear-stricken and amaz'd,
That he a rough oak trunk embrac'd,
Instead of the enchanting waist
Of his mysterious fair.

Then straight abroad a voice he heard,
Which sang the window through ;
These were the words the voice proffer'd
If my report be true :
' Come out to her whom thou didst wed !
Upon my mead thy couch is spread.'
From this he guessed with some elf maid
That he had had to do.

THE ELVES

Take heed, good people, of yourselves ;
And oh ! beware ye of the elves.

ONCE a peasant young and gay
Was in his meadow cutting hay,
There came a lovely looking lass
From out the neighbouring morass.
The lass he woo'd, her promise won,
And soon the bridal day came on.
But when the pair had got to bed,
The bridegroom found, with fear and dread,
That he a rough oak stump embrac'd,
Instead of woman's lovely waist.
Then, to increase his fear and wonder,
There sang a voice his window under :
'Come out to her whom thou didst wed,
Upon my mead the bed is spread.'
From that wild lay the peasant knew
He with a fay had had to do.

Take heed, good people, of yourselves ;
And oh ! beware ye of the elves.

THE LADY OF THE GREENWOOD

ONE summer morn, as I was seeking
My ponies in their green retreat,
I heard a lady sing a ditty
To me which sounded strangely sweet.

I am the ladye, I am the ladye,
I am the ladye loving the knight;
I in the green wood 'neath the green branches
In the night season sleep with the knight.

Since yonder summer morn of beauty
I 've seen many a gloomy year;
But in my mind still lives the ditty
That in the green wood met my ear.

I am the ladye, I am the ladye,
I am the ladye loving the knight;
I in the green wood 'neath the green branches
In the night season sleep with the knight.

THE SWORD

FULL twenty fights my father saw,
  And died with twenty red wounds gored;
I heir'd what he so loved to draw,
  His ancient silver-handled sword.

It is a sword of weight and length,
  Of jags and blood-specks nobly full;
Well wielded by his Cornish strength
  It clove the Gaulman's helm and skull.

Hurrah! thou silver-handled blade,
  Though thou 'st but little of the air
Of swords by Cornets worn on p'rade,
  To battle thee I vow to bear.

Thou 'st decked old chiefs of Cornwall's land,
  To face the fiend with thee they dared;
Thou prov'dst a Tirfing in their hand
  Which victory gave whene'er 'twas bared.

Though Cornwall's moors 'twas ne'er my lot
  To view, in Eastern Anglia born,
Yet I her sons' rude strength have got,
  And feel of death their fearless scorn.

And when the foe we have in ken,
   And with my troop I seek the fray,
Thou 'lt find the youth who wields thee then
   Will ne'er the part of Horace play.

Meanwhile above my bed's head hang,
   May no vile rust thy sides bestain ;
And soon, full soon, the war-trump's clang
   Call me and thee to glory's plain.

TO MARY ANNE

O DEARLY, sincerely
  I love thee, Mary Anne ;
More kindly, more blindly
  None love another can.

At sunrise, at moonrise
  Thou dost my bosom fill ;
When night reigns or light reigns,
  I think upon thee still.

And in Dania or Britannia
  E'en as in Petersville,
And when I am in Siam
  I 'll think upon thee still.

Coolish love is foolish love,
  Mine is hot and strong ;
Immensity, intensity,
  They both to me belong.

Though the ocean in motion
  Between so widely roll,
The needle, though little,
  Still longeth for its pole.

O'er the ocean in motion
  Still burn for thee I can ;
Then start ship and part ship
  Me from my Mary Anne.

LINES ON SEEING A POMEGRANATE IN FLOWER, FOR THE FIRST TIME, AFTER A SOJOURN IN SPAIN

Granada, sweet Granada,
  Mine eye must rest on thee,
For thou breath'st of a land of wonders,
  A clime beyond the sea.
Thou talkest of fairy visions,
  Which have vanished from my sight,
Of those bright and cloudless visions,
  Which Mem'ry clothes in light.

Thy blossoms fair remind me
  Of a bright unclouded sky,
Where 'mid orange groves I saw thee,
  With thy soft and scarlet eye.
Fair myrtles twined around thee,
  And roses of many a hue,
Thy shade has oft refreshed me,
  From its skies of dazzling blue.

Thou breath'st of Andalusia,
  And its rivers rolling slow,
Of its cypress, and acacia,
  And its black-eyed daughters too,
Of its justly famed Giralda,
  Its Delissa wild and free,
Granada, sweet Granada,
  My eye must rest on thee.

THE SHARP-TONGUED LADY

'Oh Sophy, 'tis your vile abusive tongue
That maketh everybody fear and hate you,
For dread of that no lady dares come in,
If you don't mend, you 'll kill me, Sophy Thew.'

'Mother, I 'll mend, [at] least I 'll try to do so,
But I do hate that trumpery curate Garry;
And were there not another man alive
I would not, mother, such a puppy marry—
But I will mend—but first I 'll dress for dinner.'

TO A CONCEITED WOMAN

Be still, be still, and speak not back again.
What right have you to answer in this strain?
Whilst I 'm a man, a prince of the creation,
You 're but a female woman by your station;
A creature for man's sovereign service born,
Whose fitting wages are contempt and scorn;
A creature formed to dive down in the sea
To fetch up sea-eggs for the likes of me;
Only too grateful, when we 've stilled our greed,
If on our leavings you 're allowed to feed.
If thus I speak, I speak on public grounds,
My only aim is to keep well in bounds.

A NEW SONG
TO AN OLD TUNE

WHO starves his wife,
  And denies her clothing ?
Bright the Shaker,
  The humbug Quaker !

Merrily danced the Quaker's wife,
  Merrily danced the Quaker ;
But the wife of Bright is too starved to dance,
  And he 's too fat to caper.

He grudges the wretch a morsel of food,
  He grudges her even clothing ;
Once, 'tis said, to the cupboard she stole,
  But there to steal found nothing.

But Bright's as fat as a bacon hog,
  The old outrageous sinner ;
For he will stuff at any fool's cost,
  Who 'll ask him home to dinner.

Merrily danced the Quaker's wife,
  Merrily danced the Quaker ;
But the wife of Bright is too starved to dance,
  And he 's too fat to caper.

Who starves his wife,
  And denies her clothing ?
Bright the Shaker,
  The humbug Quaker !

AND OTHER POEMS AND BALLADS

RHYMES FOR THE TIMES

No oily debaters,
No gunpowder traitors !
Hang from a garret
Gladstone and Barret !

No country betrayers,
No Royal Prince slayers !
Roll in a barrel
Bright and O'Farrel !

No philly-sophies,
Nor silly covies !
In a jakes smother
Mill and his bother !

For the black, beastly nigger
The cat with full vigour !
'Twere folly to pardon
Such villains as Gordon.

Though rogues with effrontery
Speak ill of the country,
Above it is written :
' There 's nothing like Britain ! '

May England fall never,
But flourish for ever,
In spite of all shakers
And rascally Quakers.

THE SQUINT-EYED LADY

THERE is a squint-eyed Lady,
Who in Barmouth doth reside ;
She keeps a beer-and-brandy shop,
Though she in a coach doth ride.

Outspoke the squint-eyed Lady :
'It would me much avail,
If you would but deal with me
For a single pint of ale.

'For appearances I must keep up,
Which most expensive are,
For my husband is a parson,
Although I 'm at the bar.

'And I have a son called Rufus,
And a genteel son is he,
And I cannot allow him less
A week than shillings three.

'I must give balls and concerts
And keep my coach and man ;
Therefore I pray you 'll deal with me,
As much as e'er you can.

And that you 'll recommend me
To all your kith and kin,
For I 'm not above retailing
A single glass of gin.'

Then hey for the squint-eyed Lady,
She has so little pride ;
She 'll beg for custom for her shop,
Though she in a coach doth ride.

DIABETES

In diabetes
Says the medical treatise,
You may eat
Plenty of meat,
But mustn't drink whisky,
Or wine to make you frisky,
Nor taste a drop of beer
Your heart for to cheer,
Though you may make free
With water and Bohea—
Such says the treatise
Are the rules in diabetes.

WHAT IS FAME ?

Ah, what is Fame ?
A transient flame,
A short-enduring, disappointing thing.
We can't be senior wranglers every year,
We can't be London lions every spring.

FISH

Brill, Brill, Brill
  Is a better fish than plaice.
Plaice, Plaice, Plaice
  Is the poorest of its race.

ON A YOUNG MAN WITH RED HAIR

He is a lad of sober mind,
By no means martially inclined ;
Nor fit to bear war's dreadful shocks,
Although he carries fire-locks.

DESIDERABILIA VITÆ

GIVE me the haunch of a buck to eat,
  And to drink Madeira old ;
And a gentle wife to rest with,
  And in my arms to fold.

An Arabic book to study,
  A gypsy pony to ride ;
And a house to live in shaded by trees,
  Near to a river's side.

With such good things around me,
  And with good health withal,
Though I should live for a hundred years
  For death I would not call.

AN IMPROMPTU

AND darest thou thyself compare
With one who quaffs at Helicon;
Whose playfellows the Muses are,
And whom Apollo calleth son?
Who, had he lived in olden day,
With some fierce host had strode along;
Like Taillefer to Hastings' fray,
Cheering the Normans with his song.

The laurel wreath Apollo gave
I would not change for kingly crown;
A King is but an exalted slave,
Rebellion soon may hurl him down.
But who can force me from the height
Whereto I 've soared on Eagle's wing?
I leave to Monarchs ceaseless fright
For what the coming day may bring.

Though poor I be, I 've Minstrelsy,
When fortune frowns I 'll strike my lyre;
Against the world's inclemency
'Twill warm my soul with heavenly fire.
Then wonder not, if proud the air
Of one who 's high Apollo's son;
Nor henceforth dare thyself compare
With one who quaffs at Helicon.

TO SCRIBBLERS

Would it not be more dignified
To run up debts on every side,
And then to pay your debts refuse,
Than write for rascally Reviews ?
And lectures give to great and small,
In pothouse, theatre, and town-hall,
Wearing your brains by night and day
To win the means to pay your way ?
I vow by him who reigns in [hell],
It would be more respectable !

THE LAY OF VEGTAM

'What man is he,
Unknown to me,
With reckless might
My rest doth fright?
Blown o'er by gale
And beat by hail,
By snow and rain
I long have lain.'

'I 'm Vegtam styl'd,
Am Waltham's child;
I come from far.
Now first declare
For whom so bright
Yon board is dight,
For whom foam high
The flasks I spy.'

'Of Balder dead
Behold the mead,
The fated feast
For funeral guest;
The good youths fall,
The Gods mourn all;
I speak with pain,
I 'll slumber fain.'

'Thou 'lt sleep anon :
There 's one thing, one
I seek to know
And thou must show.
Who 'll prove on plain
Young Balder's bane,
From health and joy
Hurl Odin's boy ? '

'See Hoder rear
The hateful spear.
Of Balder he
The bane shall be,
From health and joy
Hurl Odin's boy.
I speak with pain,
I 'll slumber fain.'

'Thou 'lt sleep anon :
There 's one thing, one,
All-kenner dear,
Thou 'lt deign to clear.
Who 'll vengeance call
For Balder's fall,
And Balder's foe
On beal shall throw ? '

'Rindr an heir
Shall Odin bear
Where sets the sun—
The avenging one,

He round shall roam,
His head ne'er comb,
Till Balder's foe
On beal he throw.
I speak with pain,
I 'll slumber fain.'

'Thou 'lt sleep anon:
There 's one thing, one
I seek to know
And thou must show.
Who be the maids
In yonder glades
Their locks who tear
And toss in air?'

'Alack and woe!
No Vegtam thou,
Thou Odin art
Of fearless heart.'—
'No prophetess
Art thou, I guess,
Thou mother old
Of Thurse and Trold!'

'Hie, Odin, home
Nor henceforth roam!
No wizard power
Shall wake me more
Till Lok accurst
His chain shall burst
And darkness' pall
Sink down all.'

PREFACE

THE ballads in this volume are translated from the Works of OEHLENSLÆGER, (a poet who is yet living, and who stands high in the estimation of his countrymen,) and from the KIÆMPÉ VISER, a collection of old songs, celebrating the actions of the ancient heroes of Scandinavia.

The old Danish poets were, for the most part, extremely rude in their versification. Their stanzas of four or two lines have not the full rhyme of vowel and consonant, but merely what the Spaniards call the 'assonante,' or vowel rhyme, and attention seldom seems to have been paid to the number of *feet* on which the lines moved along. But, however defective their poetry may be in point of harmony of numbers, it describes, in vivid and barbaric language, scenes of barbaric grandeur, which in these days are never witnessed; and, which, though the modern muse may imagine, she generally fails in attempting to pourtray, from the violent desire to be smooth and tuneful, forgetting that smoothness and tunefulness are nearly synonymous with tameness and unmeaningness.

I expect shortly to lay before the public a

complete translation of the KIÆMPÉ VISER, made by me some years ago; and of which, I hope, the specimens here produced will not give an unfavourable idea.

It was originally my intention to publish, among the 'Miscellaneous Pieces,' several translations from the Gælic, formerly the language of the western world; the noble tongue

'A labhair Padric 'nninse Fail na Riogh,
'San faighe caomhsin Colum náomhta 'n I.'

Which Patrick spoke in Innisfail, to heathen chiefs of old;
Which Columb, the mild prophet-saint, spoke in his island-hold—

but I have retained them, with one exception, till I possess a sufficient quantity to form an entire volume.

[Facsimile of
the original Title Page.
200 copies by subscription.]

ROMANTIC BALLADS,

TRANSLATED FROM THE DANISH;

AND

MISCELLANEOUS PIECES;

BY

GEORGE BORROW.

Through gloomy paths unknown—
Paths which untrodden be,
From rock to rock I roam
Along the dashing sea.

BOWRING.

NORWICH:

PRINTED AND PUBLISHED BY S. WILKIN, UPPER HAYMARKET.

1826.

[Facsimile of
the second London Title Page.
300 copies including those bearing the imprint of
John Taylor.]

ROMANTIC BALLADS,

TRANSLATED FROM THE DANISH;

AND

MISCELLANEOUS PIECES;

BY

GEORGE BORROW.

Through gloomy paths unknown—
Paths which untrodden be,
From rock to rock I roam
Along the dashing sea.

BOWRING.

LONDON:
PUBLISHED BY WIGHTMAN AND CRAMP,
24, PATERNOSTER ROW.

1826.

[Facsimile of
the London (John Taylor) Title Page.
300 copies including those bearing the imprint of
Wightman & Cramp.]

ROMANTIC BALLADS,

TRANSLATED FROM THE DANISH;

AND

MISCELLANEOUS PIECES;

BY

GEORGE BORROW.

Through gloomy paths unknown—
 Paths which untrodden be,
From rock to rock I roam
 Along the dashing sea.

BOWRING.

LONDON:
JOHN TAYLOR, WATERLOO PLACE, PALL MALL.

1826.

FROM

ALLAN CUNNINGHAM, TO GEORGE BORROW,

On his proposing to translate the 'Kiœmpé Viser.'

SING, sing, my friend; breathe life again
Through Norway's song and Denmark's strain:
On flowing Thames and Forth, in flood,
Pour Haco's war-song, fierce and rude.
O'er England's strength, through Scotland's cold,
His warrior minstrels marched of old—
Called on the wolf and bird of prey
To feast on Ireland's shore and bay;
And France, thy forward knights and bold,
Rough Rollo's ravens croaked them cold.
Sing, sing of earth and ocean's lords,
Their songs as conquering as their swords;
Strains, steeped in many a strange belief,
Now stern as steel, now soft as grief—
Wild, witching, warlike, brief, sublime,
Stamped with the image of their time;
When chafed—the call is sharp and high
For carnage, as the eagles cry;
When pleased—the mood is meek, and mild,
And gentle, as an unweaned child.
Sing, sing of haunted shores and shelves,
St. Oluf and his spiteful elves,

Of that wise dame, in true love need,
Who of the clear stream formed the steed—
How youthful Svend, in sorrow sharp,
The inspired strings rent from his harp ;
And Sivard, in his cloak of felt,
Danced with the green oak at his belt—
Or sing the Sorceress of the wood,
The amorous Merman of the flood—
Or elves that, o'er the unfathomed stream,
Sport thick as motes in morning beam—
Or bid me sail from Iceland Isle,
With Rosmer and fair Ellenlyle,
What time the blood-crow's flight was south,
Bearing a man's leg in its mouth.
Though rough and rude, those strains are rife
Of things kin to immortal life,
Which touch the heart and tinge the cheek,
As deeply as divinest Greek.
In simple words and unsought rhyme,
Give me the songs of olden time.

THE DEATH-RAVEN.

FROM THE DANISH OF OEHLENSLÆGER.

THE silken sail, which caught the summer breeze,
Drove the light vessel through the azure seas;
Upon the lofty deck, Dame Sigrid lay,
And watch'd the setting of the orb of day:
Then, all at once, the smiling sky grew dark,
The breakers rav'd, and sinking seem'd the bark;
The wild Death-raven, perch'd upon the mast,
Scream'd 'mid the tumult, and awoke the blast.

Dame Sigrid saw the demon bird on high,
And tear-drops started in her beauteous eye;
Her cheeks, which late like blushing roses bloom'd
Had now the pallid hue of fear assum'd:
'O wild death-raven, calm thy frightful rage,
Nor war with one who warfare cannot wage.
Tame yonder billows, make them cease to roar,
And I will give thee pounds of golden ore.'

'With gold thou must not hope to pay the brave,
For gold I will not calm a single wave,
For gold I will not hush the stormy air,
And yet my heart is mov'd by thy despair;
Give me the treasure hid beneath thy belt,
And straight yon clouds in harmless rain shall melt,
And down I 'll thunder, with my claws of steel,
Upon the merman clinging to your keel.'

'What I conceal'd beneath my girdle bear,
Is thine—irrevocably thine—I swear.
Thou hast refus'd a great and noble prey,
To get possession of my closet key.
Lo! here it is, and, when within thy maw,
May'st thou much comfort from the morsel draw!'
The polish'd steel upon the deck she cast,
And off the raven flutter'd from the mast.

Then down at once he plung'd amid the main,
And clove the merman's frightful head in twain;
The foam-clad billows to repose he brought,
And tam'd the tempest with the speed of thought;
Then, with a thrice-repeated demon cry,
He soar'd aloft and vanish'd in the sky:
A soft wind blew the ship towards the land,
And soon Dame Sigrid reach'd the wish'd-for
strand.

Once, late at eve, she play'd upon her harp,
Close by the lake where slowly swam the carp;
And, as the moon-beam down upon her shone,
She thought of Norway, and its pine-woods lone.
'Yet love I Denmark,' said she, 'and the Danes,
For o'er them Alf, my mighty husband, reigns.'
Then 'neath her girdle something mov'd and
yearn'd,
And into terror all her bliss was turn'd.

'Ah! now I know thy meaning, cruel bird. . . .'
Long sat she, then, and neither spoke nor stirr'd.
Faint, through the mist which rob'd the sky in gray,
The pale stars glimmer'd from the milky way.

'Ah! now I know thy meaning, cruel bird . . .'
She strove in vain to breathe another word.
Above her head, its leaf the aspen shook—
Moist as her cheek, and pallid as her look.

Full five months pass'd, ere she, 'mid night and gloom,
Brought forth with pain an infant from her womb:
They baptiz'd it, at midnight's murky hour,
Lest it should fall within the demon's power.
It was a boy, more lovely than the morn,
Yet Sigrid's heart with bitter care was torn.
Deep in a grot, through which a brook did flow,
With crystal drops they sprinkled Harrald's brow.

He grew and grew, till upon Danish ground
No youth to match the stripling could be found;
He was at once so graceful and so strong—
His look was fire, and his speech was song.
When yet a child, he tam'd the battle steed,
And only thought of war and daring deed;
But yet Queen Sigrid nurs'd prophetic fears,
And when she view'd him, always swam in tears.

One evening late, she lay upon her bed,
(King Alf, her noble spouse, was long since dead)
She felt so languid, and her aching breast
With more than usual sorrow was oppress'd.
Ah, then she heard a sudden sound that thrill'd
Her every nerve, and life's warm current chill'd:—
The bird of death had through the casement flown,
And thus he scream'd to her, in frightful tone:

'The wealthy bird came towering,
Came scowering,
O'er hill and stream.
" Look here, look here, thou needy bird,
How gay my feathers gleam."

'The needy bird came fluttering,
Came muttering,
And sadly sang,
" Look here, look here, thou wealthy bird,
How loose my feathers hang."

'Remember, Queen, the stormy day,
When cast away
Thou wast so nigh :—
Thou wast the needy bird that day,
And unto me didst cry.
Death-raven now comes towering,
Comes scowering,
O'er hill and stream ;
But when wilt thou, Dame Sigrid fair,
Thy plighted word redeem.'

A hollow moan from Sigrid's bosom came,
While he survey'd her with his eye of flame :
'Fly,' said she ; 'demon monster, get thee hence !
My humble pray'r shall be my son's defence.'
She cross'd herself, and then the fiend flew out ;
But first, contemptuously he danc'd about,
And sang, 'No pray'r shall save him from my rage ;
In Christian blood my thirst I will assuage.'

Young Harrald seiz'd his scarlet cap, and cried,
'I'll probe the grief my mother fain would hide';
Then, rushing into her apartment fair,
'O mother,' said he, 'wherefore sitt'st thou there,
Far from thy family at dead of night,
With lips so mute, and cheeks so ghastly white?
Tell me what lies so heavy at thy heart;
Grief, when confided, loses half its smart.'

'O Harrald,' sigh'd she, yielding to his pray'r,
'Creatures are swarming in the earth and air,
Who, wild with wickedness, and hot with wrath,
Wage war on those who follow virtue's path.
One of those fiends is on the watch for thee,
Arm'd with a promise wrung by him from me:
His blood-shot eyes in narrow sockets roll,
And every night he leaves his mirksome hole.

'He was a kind of God, in former days;
Kings worshipp'd him, and minstrels sang his praise;
But when Christ's doctrine through the dark North flam'd,
His, and all evil spirits' might was tam'd.
He now is but a raven; yet is still
Full strong enough to work on thee his will:
Lost is the wretch who in his power falls —
Vainly he shrieks, in vain for mercy calls.'

She whisper'd to him then, with bloodless lip,
What had befallen her on board the ship;
But youthful Harrald listen'd undismay'd,
And merely gripp'd the handle of his blade.

'My son,' she murmur'd, when her tale was told,
'Fear withers me, but thou look'st blythe and
bold.'
The youth uplifted then his sparkling eye,
And said, whilst gazing on the moon-lit sky,

'Once, my dear mother, at the close of day,
Among tall flowers in the grove I lay,
Soft sang the linnets from a thousand trees,
And, sweetly lull'd, I slumber'd by degrees.
Then, heaven's curtain was, methought, undrawn,
And, clad in hues that deck the brow of morn,
An angel slowly sank towards the earth,
Which seem'd to hail him with a smile of mirth.

'He rais'd his hand, and bade me fix my eye
Upon a chain which, hanging from the sky,
Embrac'd the world; and, stretching high and
low,
Clink'd, as it mov'd, the notes of joy and wo:
The links that came in sight were purpled o'er
Full frequently with what seem'd human gore;
Of various metals made, it clasp'd the mould,—
Steel clung to silver, iron clung to gold.

'Then said the angel, with majestic air,—
"The chain of destiny thou seest there.
Accept whate'er it gives, and murmur not;
For hard necessity has cast each lot."
He vanish'd—I awoke with sudden start,
But that strange dream was graven on my heart.
I go wherever fate shall please to call,—
Without God's leave, no fly to earth can fall.'

It thunders—and from midnight's mirky cloud,
Comes peal on peal reverberating loud :
The froth-clad breakers cast, with sullen roar,
A Scottish bark upon the whiten'd shore.
Straight to the royal palace hasten then
A lovely maid and thirty sea-worn men.
Minona, Scotland's princess, Scotland's boast,
The storm has driven to the Danish coast.

Oft, while the train hew timber in the groves,
Minona, arm in arm, with Harrald roves.
Warm from his lip the words of passion flow ;
Pure in her eyes the flames of passion glow.
One summer eve, upon a mossy bank,
Mouth join'd to mouth, and breast to breast, they sank :
The moon arose in haste to see their love,
And wild birds carroll'd from the boughs above.

But now the ship, which seem'd of late a wreck,
Floats with a mast set proudly on her deck.
Minona kisses Harrald's blooming face,
Whilst he attends her to the parting place.
His bold young heart beats high against his side—
She sail'd away—and, like one petrified,
Full long he stood upon the shore, to view
The smooth keel slipping through the waters blue.

Months pass, and Sigrid's sorrow disappears ;
The wild death-raven's might no more she fears ;
A gentle red bedecks her cheek again,
And briny drops her eye no longer stain.

'My Harrald stalks in manly size and strength;
Swart bird of darkness, I rejoice at length;
If thy curst claw could hurt my gallant son,
Long, long, ere this, the deed would have been done.'

But Harrald look'd so moody and forlorn,
And thus his mother he address'd one morn:
'Minona's face is equall'd by her mind;
Methinks she calls me from her hills of wind?
Give me a ship with men and gold at need,
And let me to her father's kingdom speed;
I'll soon return, and back across the tide
Bring thee a daughter, and myself a bride.'

Dame Sigrid promis'd him an answer soon,
And went that night, when risen was the moon,
Deep through the black recesses of the wood,
To where old Bruno's shelter'd cabin stood.
She enter'd—there he sat behind his board,
His woollen vestment girded by a cord;
The little lamp, which hung from overhead,
Gleam'd on the Bible-leaves before him spread.

'Hail to thee, Father!—man of hoary age,
Thy Queen demands from thee thy counsel sage.
Young Harrald to a distant land will go,
And I his destiny would gladly know:
Thou read'st the stars,—O do the stars portend
That he shall come to an untimely end?
Take from his mother's heart this one last care,
And she will always name thee in her pray'r.'

The hermit, rising from his lonely nook,
With naked head, and coldly placid look,
Went out and gaz'd intently on the sky,
Whose lights were letters to his ancient eye.
'The stars,' said he, 'in friendly order stand,
One only, flashes like an angry brand :—
Thy Harrald, gentle Queen, will not be slain
Upon the *Earth*, nor yet upon the *Main*.'

While thus the seer prophetically spoke,
A flush of joy o'er Sigrid's features broke :
'He 'll not be slain on ocean or on land,'
She said, and kiss'd the hermit's wrinkled hand ;
'Why then, I 'm happy, and my son is free
To mount his bark, and gallop through the sea :
Upon the grey stone he will sit as king,
When, in the grave, my bones are mouldering.'

The painted galley floats now in the creek—
Flags at her mast, and garlands at her beak ;
High on the yard-arm hoisted is the sail,
Half spread it flutters in the evening gale.
The night before he goes, young Harrald stray'd
Into the wood where first he saw his maid :
Burning impatience fever'd all his blood,
He wish'd for wings to bear him o'er the flood.

Then sigh'd the wind among the bushy grounds,
Far in the distance rose the yell of hounds :
The flame-wisps, starting from the sedge and grass,
Hung, 'mid the vapours, over the morass.

Up to him came a beldame, wildly drest,
Bearing a closely-folded feather-vest :
She smil'd upon him with her cheeks so wan,
Gave him the robe, and was already gone.

Young Harrald, though astonish'd, has no fears ;
The mighty garment in his hand he rears :
Of wond'rous lovely feathers it was made,
Which once the roc and ostrich had array'd.
He wishes much to veil in it his form,
And speed as rapidly as speeds the storm :
He puts it on, then seeks the open plain,—
Takes a short flight, and flutters back again.

'Courage ! ' he cried, 'I will no longer stay ;
Scotland shall see me, ere the break of day.'
Then like a dragon in the air he soars,
Startled from slumber, in his wake it roars.
His wings across the ocean take their flight ;
Groves, cities, hills, have vanish'd from his sight,—
See ! there he goes, lone rider of the sky,
Miles underneath him, black the billows lie.

He hears a clapping on the midnight wind :
Speed, Harrald, speed ! the raven is behind.
Flames from his swarthy-rolling eye are cast :—
'Ha ! Harrald,' scream'd he, 'have we met at last ? '
For the first time, the youth felt terror's force ;
Pale grew his cheek, as that of clammy corse,
Chill was his blood, his nervous arm was faint,
While thus he stammer'd forth his lowly plaint :

'I see it is in vain to strive with fate;
Thank God, my soul is far above thy hate;
But, ere my mortal part thou dost destroy,
Let me one moment of sweet bliss enjoy:
The fair unmatch'd Minona is my love,
For her I travell'd, fool-like, here above:
Let me fly to her with my last farewell,
And I am thine, ere morning decks the fell.'

Firmly the raven holding him in air,
Survey'd his prize with fiercely-rabid glare:
'Now is the time to wreak on thee my lust;
Yet thou shalt own that I am good and just.'
Then from its socket, Harrald's eye he tore,
And drank a full half of the hero's gore:—
'Since I have mark'd thee, thou art free to go;
But loiter not when thou art there below.'

Young Harrald sinks with many a sob and tear,
Down from the sky to nature's lower sphere:
He rested long beneath the poplar tall,
Which grew up, under the red church's wall.
Then, rising slow, he feebly stagger'd on,
Till his Minona's bower he had won.
Trembling and sad he stood beside the door—
Pale as a spectre, and besprent with gore!

'Minona, come, ere Harrald's youthful heart
Is burst by love and complicated smart.
Soon will his figure disappear from earth,
Yet we shall meet in heaven's halls of mirth:

Minona, come and give me one embrace,
That I may instantly my path retrace.'
Thus warbles he in passion's wildest note,
While death each moment rattles in his throat.

Minona came : ' Almighty God ! ' she cried,
' My Harrald's ghost has wander'd o'er the tide ;
Red clots of blood his yellow tresses streak,
Drops of the same are running down his cheek.'
' Minona, love, survey me yet more near,
It is no shadow which accosts thee here ;
Place thy warm hand upon my heart, and feel
Whether it beats for thee with slacken'd zeal.'

At once the current of her tears she stopp'd,
His arm upheld her, or the maid had dropp'd ;
The roses faded from her face away,
And on her head the raven locks grew gray.
All he had borne, and what he yet must bear,
He murmurs to her whilst she trembles there :
The hero then with dying ardour press'd,
For the last time, his bosom to her breast.

' Farewell ! Minona, all my fears are flown,
And if I grieve, it is for thee alone :
Give me a kiss, and give me too a smile,
And let not tears that parting look defile.
Now will I drink the bitter draught of death,
And yield courageously my forfeit breath :—
Farewell ! may heaven take thee in its care,'
He said, and mounted swiftly in the air.

She gaz'd ; but he had vanish'd from her view ;
She stood forsaken in the damp and dew.
Then dark emotion quiver'd in her eye,
And thus she pray'd, with hands uplifted high :
'Thou who wert vainly tempted in the wild,
Thou who wert always charitably mild,
Thou who mad'st Peter walk on billows blue,
Enable me my Harrald to pursue.'

Sunken already was the morning star,
The song of nightingales was heard afar,
The red sun peep'd above the mountain's brow,
And flowers scented all the vale below.
There came a youthful maiden, gaily drest,
Bearing upon her back a feather-vest ;
Fondly she kiss'd Minona's features wan,
Gave her the robe, and then at once was gone.

And straight Minona clothes in it her limbs,
And soaring upward through the ether swims :
To moan and sob, her madden'd breast disdains,
Too big for such low comfort are its pains.
The fowls that meet her in yon airy fields,
She clips in pieces with an axe she wields ;
Each clanging pinion ceaselessly she plies,
But cannot meet the raven or his prize.

She hears a faint shriek in the air below,
And, swift as eagle pounces on his foe,
Down, down, she dropp'd, and lighted on the shore,
Which far and wide was wet with Harrald's gore.

She smil'd so ruefully, but still was mute—
His good right hand was lying at her foot :
That pledge of truth, in love's unclouded day,
Was the sole remnant of the demon's prey.

Deep in her breast she hid the bloody hand,
And bade adieu, for ever, to the land :
Again she scower'd through the airy path,
Her eyeballs terrible with madden'd wrath :
The raven-sorcerer at length she spied,
And soon her steel was with his hot blood dyed :
The huge black body, piecemeal, found a grave
Amid the bosom of the briny wave.

The ocean billows fret and foam no more,
But softly rush towards the pebbled shore,
On which the lindens stand, in many a group,
With leafy boughs that o'er the waters droop.
There floats one single cloudlet in the blue,
Close where the pale moon shows her face anew :
It is Minona dying there that flies,—
She sinks not !—no—she mounts unto the skies.

FRIDLEIF AND HELGA.

FROM THE DANISH OF OEHLENSLÆGER.

THE woods were in leaf, and they cast a sweet shade;
Among them walk'd Helga, the beautiful maid.

The water is dashing o'er yon little stones;
She sat down beside it, and rested her bones.

She sat down, and soon, from a bush that was near,
Sir Fridleif approach'd her with sword and with spear:

'Ah, pity me, Helga, and fly me not now,
I live, only live, on the smile of thy brow:

'In thy father's whole garden is found not a rose,
Which bright as thyself, and as beautiful grows.'

'Sir Fridleif, thy words are but meant to deceive,
Yet tell me what brings thee so late here at eve.'

'I cannot find rest, and I cannot find ease,
Though sweet sing the linnets among the wild trees;

'If thou wilt but promise, one day to be mine,
No more shall I sorrow, no more shall I pine.'

She sank in his arms, and her cheeks were as red
As the sun when he sinks in his watery bed ;

But soon she arose from his loving embrace ;
He walk'd by her side, through the wood, for a
space.

' Now listen, young Fridleif, the gallant and bold,
Take off from my finger this ring of red gold,

Take off from my finger this ring of red gold,
And part with it not, till in death thou art cold.'

Sir Fridleif stood there in a sorrowful plight,
Salt tears wet his eyeballs, and blinded his sight.

' Go home, and I 'll come to thy father with speed,
And claim thee from him, on my mighty grey
steed.'

Sir Fridleif, at night, through the thick forest rode,
He fain would arrive at his lov'd one's abode ;

His harness was clanking, his helm glitter'd sheen,
His horse was so swift, and himself was so keen :

He reach'd the proud castle, and jump'd on the
ground,
His horse to the branch of a linden he bound ;

He shoulder'd his mantle of grey otter skin,
And through the wide door, to Sir Erik went in.

' Here sitt'st thou, Sir Erik, in scarlet array'd ;
I 've wedded thy daughter, the beautiful maid.'

'And who art thou, Rider? what feat hast thou
done?
No nidering coward shall e'er be my son.'

'O far have I wander'd, renown'd is my name,
The heroes I conquer'd wherever I came:

'Han Elland, 'tis true, long disputed the ground,
But yet he receiv'd from my hand his death-
wound.'

Sir Erik then alter'd his countenance quite,
And out hurried he, in the gloom of the night.

'Fill high, little Kirstin, my best drinking cup,
And be the brown liquor with poison mixt up.'

She gave him the draught, and returning with
speed,
'Young gallant,' said he, 'thou must taste my
old mead.'

Sir Fridleif unbuckled his helmet and drank;
Sweat sprung from his forehead—his features
grew blank.

'I never have drain'd, since the day I was born,
A bitterer draught, from a costlier horn:

'My course is completed, my life is summ'd up,
For treason I smell in the dregs of the cup.'

Sir Erik then said, while he stamp'd on the
ground,
'Young knight, 'tis thy fortune to die like a hound.

'My best belov'd friend thou didst boast to have slain,
And I have aveng'd him by giving thee bane:

'Not Helga, but Hela,[1] shall now be thy bride;
Dark blue are her cheeks, and she looks stony-eyed.'

'Sir Erik, thy words are both witty and wise,
And hell, when it has thee, will have a rich prize!

'Convey unto Helga her gold ring so red;
Be sure to inform her when Fridleif is dead;

'But flame shall give water, and marble shall bleed,
Before thou shalt win by this treacherous deed:

'And I will not die like a hound, in the straw,
But go, like a hero, to Odin and Thor.'

He cut himself thrice, with his keen-cutting glaive,
And went to Valhalla,[2] the way of the brave.

The knight bade his daughter come into the room:
'Look here, my sweet child, on thy merry bride-groom.'

She look'd on the body, and gave a wild start;
'O father, why hadst thou so cruel a heart?'

She moan'd and lamented, she rav'd and she curst;
She look'd on her love, till her very eyes burst.

[1] The goddess of death—according to the Northern mythology

[2] The paradise of the Northern mythology.

At midnight, Sir Erik was standing there mute,
With two pallid corses beside his cold foot :

He stood stiff and still ; and when morning-light
came,
He stood, like a post, without life in his frame.

The youth and the maid were together interr'd,
Sir Erik could not from his posture be stirr'd :

He stood there, as stiffly, for thirty long days,
And look'd on the earth with a petrified gaze.

'Tis said, on the night of the thirtieth long day,
To dust and to ashes he moulder'd away.

SIR MIDDEL.

FROM THE OLD DANISH.

So tightly was Swanelil lacing her vest,
That forth spouted milk, from each lily-white breast;
That saw the Queen-mother, and thus she begun:
'What maketh the milk from thy bosom to run?'
'O this is not milk, my dear mother, I vow;
It is but the mead I was drinking just now.'
'Ha! out on thee minion! these eyes have their sight;
Would'st tell me that mead, in its colour, is white?'
'Well, well, since the proofs are so glaring and strong,
I own that Sir Middel has done me a wrong.'
'And was he the miscreant? dear shall he pay,
For the cloud he has cast on our honour's bright ray;
I'll hang him up; yes, I will hang him with scorn,
And burn thee to ashes, at breaking of morn.'
The maiden departed in anguish and wo,
And straight to Sir Middel it lists her to go;
Arriv'd at the portal, she sounded the bell,
'Now wake thee, love, if thou art living and well.'
Sir Middel he heard her, and sprang from his bed;
Not knowing her voice, in confusion he said,

'Away: for I have neither candle nor light,
And I swear that no mortal shall enter this night!'
'Now busk ye, Sir Middel, in Christ's holy name;
I fly from my mother, who knows of my shame;
She'll hang thee up; yes, she will hang thee with scorn,
And burn me to ashes, at breaking of morn.'
'Ha! laugh at her threat'nings, so empty and wild;
She neither shall hang me, nor burn thee, my child:
Collect what is precious, in jewels and garb,
And I'll to the stable and saddle my barb.'
He gave her the cloak, that he us'd at his need,
And he lifted her up, on the broad-bosom'd steed.
The forest is gain'd, and the city is past,
When her eyes to the heaven she wistfully cast.
'What ails thee, dear maid? we had better now stay,
For thou art fatigu'd by the length of the way.'
'I am not fatigu'd by the length of the way;
But my seat is uneasy, in truth, I must say.'
He spread, on the cold earth, his mantle so wide;
'Now rest thee, my love, and I'll watch by thy side.'
'O Jesus, that one of my maidens were near!
The pains of a mother are on me, I fear.'
'Thy maidens are now at a distance from thee,
And thou art alone in the forest with me.'
''Twere better to perish, again and again,
Than thou should'st stand by me, and gaze on my pain.'

‘ Then take off thy kerchief, and cover my head,
And perhaps I may stand in the wise-woman’s stead.’
‘ O Christ, that I had but a draught of the wave !
To quench my death-thirst, and my temples to lave.’
Sir Middel was to her so tender and true,
And he fetch’d her the drink in her gold-spangled shoe.
The fountain was distant, and when he drew near,
Two nightingales sat there and sang in his ear :
‘ Thy love, she is dead, and for ever at rest,
With two little babes that lie cold on her breast.’
Such was their song ; but he heeded them not,
And trac’d his way back to the desolate spot ;
But oh, what a spectacle burst on his view !
For all they had told him was fatally true.
He dug a deep grave by the side of a tree,
And buried therein the unfortunate three.
As he clamp’d the mould down with his iron-heel’d boot,
He thought that the babies scream’d under his foot :
Then placing his weapon against a grey stone,
He cast himself on it, and died with a groan.
Ye maidens of Norway, henceforward beware !
For love, when unbridled, will end in despair.

ROMANTIC BALLADS

ELVIR-SHADES.

FROM THE DANISH OF OEHLENSLÆGER.

A SULTRY eve pursu'd a sultry day ;
Dark streaks of purple in the sky were seen,
And shadows half conceal'd the lonely way ;

I spurr'd my courser, and more swiftly rode,
In moody silence, through the forests green,
Where doves and linnets had their lone abode :

It was my fate to reach a brook, at last,
Which, by sweet-scented bushes fenc'd around,
Defiance bade to heat and nipping blast.

Inclin'd to rest, and hear the wild birds' song,
I stretch'd myself upon that brook's soft bound,
And there I fell asleep and slumber'd long ;

And only woke, O wonder, to perceive
A gold-hair'd maiden, as a snowdrop pale,
Her slender form from out the ground upheave :

Then fear o'ercame me, and this daring heart
Beat three times audibly against my mail ;
I wish'd to speak, but could no sound impart.

And see ! another maid rose up and took
Some drops of water from the foaming rill,
And gaz'd upon me with a wistful look.

Said she, ' What brings thee to this lonely place ?
But do not fear, for thou shalt meet no ill ;
Thou steel-clad warrior, full of youth and grace.'

' No ; ' sang the other, in delightful tone,
' But thou shalt gaze on prodigies which ne'er
To man's unhallow'd eye have yet been shown.'

The brook which lately brawl'd among the trees
Stood still, the murmur of that song to hear ;
No green leaf stirr'd, and fetter'd seem'd the breeze.

The thrush, upstarting in the distant dell,
Shook its brown wing, with golden streaks array'd,
And ap'd the witch-notes, as they rose and fell.

Bright gleam'd the lake's broad sheet of liquid blue,
Where, with the rabid pike, the troutling play'd ;
The rose unlock'd its folded leaves anew,

And blush'd, besprinkled with the night's cold tear.
Once more the lily rais'd its head and smil'd,
All ghastly white, as when it decks the bier.

Though sweet she sang, my fears were not the less,
For in her accents there was something wild,
Which I can feel, 'tis true, but not express.

' Come with us,' sang she, ' deep below the earth,
Where sun ne'er burns, and storm-winds never rave ;
Come with us to our halls of princely mirth,

'There thou shalt learn from us the Runic lay;
But dip thee, first, in yonder crystal wave,
Which binds thee to the Elfin race for aye:

'Though painted flowers on earth's breast abound,
Yet we have far more lovely ones below;
Like grass the chrysolites there strew the ground.'

'O come,' the other syren did exclaim,
'For rubies there more red than roses grow—
The sapphir's blue the violet puts to shame.'

I rais'd my eyes to heaven's starry dome,
And gripp'd my faulchion with convulsive might,
Resolv'd no witchcraft should my mind o'ercome.

My lengthen'd silence vex'd the maidens sore:
'Wilt thou detain us here the live-long night,
Or must we, stripling, proffer something more?

'Taught by us, thou shalt bind the rugged bear,—
Seize on the mighty dragon's heap of gold,—
And slay the cockatrice while in her lair!

'But from thy breast the blood we will suck out,
Unless thou follow us beneath the mould!
Decide, decide, nor longer pause in doubt!'

Cold sweat I shed, and as, with trembling hand,
I strove to whirl my beaming faulchion round,
It sank, enthrall'd by magic's potent band.

Each witch drew nigh, with dagger high up-
rear'd ;
Just then a cock, beyond the wild wood's bound,
Crew loud—and in the earth they disappear'd.

I flung myself upon my frighten'd barb,
Just as the shades began to grow less murk,
And sun-beams clad the sky in gayer garb.

Let each young warrior from such places fly :
Disease and death beneath the flowers lurk ;
And elves would suck the warm blood from his
eye.

ROMANTIC BALLADS

THE HEDDYBEE-SPECTRE.

FROM THE OLD DANISH.

I CLOMB in haste my dappled steed,
And gallop'd far o'er mount and mead ;
And when the day drew nigh its close,
I laid me down to take repose.

I laid me down to take repose,
And slumbers sweet fell o'er my brows :
And then, methought, as there I slept,
From out the ground the dead man leapt.

Said he, ' If thou art valiant, Knight,
My murder soon will see the light ;
For thou wilt ride to Heddybee,
Where live my youthful brothers three :

' And there, too, thou wilt surely find
My father dear and mother kind ;
And there sits Kate, my much-loved wife,
Who with her women took my life.

' They chok'd me, as in bed I lay,
Then wrapp'd me in a truss of hay ;
And bore me out at dead of night,
And laid me in this lonely height.

'The Groom, who lately clean'd my stall,
Now struts and vapours through my hall,—
Eats gaily with my silver knife,
And sleeps with Kate, my much-lov'd wife.

'His place is highest at the board;
But what is most to be deplor'd,
He gives my babes so little bread,
And mocks them now their sire is dead.

'Clad in my clothes he proudly stalks
Along the shady forest-walks;
And, arm'd with bow and hunting spear,
He shoots my birds and stabs my deer.

'Were I alive, to meet him now,
All underneath the linden bough,
With no one nigh, my wrath to check,
I'd wring his head from off his neck!

'But hie thee hence to Heddybee,
Where live my youthful brothers three;
First tell them all—then stab the groom—
Allow my wife a milder doom.'

SIR JOHN.

FROM THE OLD DANISH.

Sir Lavé to the island stray'd ;
He wedded there a lovely maid :
' I 'll have her yet,' said John.

He brought her home across the main,
With knights and ladies in the train :
' I 'm close behind,' said John.

They plac'd her on the bridal seat ;
Sir Lavé bade them drink and eat :
' Aye : that we will,' said John.

The servants led her then to bed,
But could not loose her girdle red !
' I can, perhaps,' said John.

He shut the door with all his might ;
He lock'd it fast, and quench'd the light :
' I shall sleep here,' said John.

A servant to Sir Lavé hied ;—
' Sir John is sleeping with the bride : '
' Aye, that I am,' said John.

Sir Lavé to the chamber flew :
' Arise, and straight the door undo ! '
' A likely thing ! ' said John.

He struck with shield, he struck with spear—
' Come out, thou Dog, and fight me here ! '
' Another time,' said John.

'And since thou with my bride hast lain,
To our good king I will complain.'
'That thou canst do,' said John.

As soon as e'er the morning shone,
Sir Lavé sought our monarch's throne;
'I 'll go there too,' said John.

'O King, chastise this wicked wight,
For with my wife he slept last night.'
''Tis very true,' said John.

'Since ye two love one pretty face,
Your lances must decide the case.'
'With all my heart,' said John.

The sun on high was shining bright,
And thousands came to see the fight:
'Lo! here I am,' said John.

The first course that they ran so free,
Sir John's horse fell upon his knee:
'Now help me God!' said John.

The next course that they ran, in ire,
Sir Lavé fell among the mire.
'He 's dead enough!' said John.

The victor to the castle hied,
And there in tears he found the bride:
'Thou art my own,' said John.

That night, forgetting all alarms,
Again she blest him in her arms.
'I have her now!' said John.

ROMANTIC BALLADS

MAY [1] ASDA.

FROM THE DANISH OF OEHLENSLÆGER

May Asda is gone to the merry green wood;
Like flax was each tress on her temples that stood;
Her cheek like the rose-leaf that perfumes the air;
Her form, like the lily-stalk, graceful and fair:

She mourn'd for her lover, Sir Frovin the brave,
For he had embark'd on the boisterous wave;
And, burning to gather the laurels of war,
Had sail'd with King Humble to Orkney afar:

At feast and at revel, wherever she went,
Her thoughts on his perils and dangers were bent;
No joy has the heart that loves fondly and dear—
No pleasure save when the lov'd object is near!

May Asda walk'd out in the bonny noon-tide,
And roam'd where the beeches grew up in their pride;
She sat herself down on the green sloping hill,
Where liv'd the Erl-people,[2] and where they live still:

[1] Moe in Danish signifies Maid, and is pronounced nearly like 'May.' May is Old English for Maid.

[2] The Fairies.—Ellefolk. *Dan.*

Then trembled the turf, as she sat in repose,
And straight from the mountain three maidens arose;
And with them a loom, and upon it a woof,
As white as the snow when it falls on the roof.

Of red shining gold was the fairy-loom made;
They sang and they danc'd, and their swift shuttles play'd;
Their song was of death, and their song was of life,
It sounded like billows in tumult and strife.

They gave her the woof, with a sorrowful look,
And vanish'd like bubbles that burst on the brook;
But deep in the mountain was heard a sweet strain,
As the lady went home to her bower again.

The web was unfinish'd; she wove and she spun,
Nor rested a moment, until it was done;
And there was enough, when the work was complete,
To form for a dead man a shirt or a sheet.

The heroes return'd from the well-foughten field,
And bore home Sir Frovin's corse, laid on a shield;
Sad sight for the maid! but she still was alert,
And sew'd round the body the funeral shirt:

And when she had come to the very last stitch,
Her feelings, so long suppress'd, rose to a pitch,
The cold clammy sweat from her features out-
broke ;
Death struck her, and meekly she bow'd to the
stroke.

She rests with her lover now deep in the grave,
And o'er them the beeches their mossy boughs
wave ;
There sing the Erl-maidens their ditties aloud,
And dance while the merry moon peeps from the
cloud.

AAGER AND ELIZA.

FROM THE OLD DANISH.

Have ye heard of bold Sir Aager,
How he rode to yonder isle ;
There he saw the sweet Eliza,
Who upon him deign'd to smile.

There he married sweet Eliza,
With her lands and ruddy gold—
Wo is me ! the Monday after,
Dead he lay beneath the mould !

In her bower sat Eliza ;
Rent the air with shriek and groan ;
All which heard the good Sir Aager,
Underneath the granite stone.

Up his mighty limbs he gather'd,
Took the coffin on his back ;
And to fair Eliza's bower
Hasten'd, by the well-known track.

On her chamber's lowly portal,
With his fingers long and thin,
Thrice he tapp'd, and bade Eliza
Straightway let her bridegroom in !

Straightway answer'd fair Eliza,
'I will not undo my door
Till I hear thee name sweet Jesus,
As thou oft hast done before.'

'Rise, O rise, my own Eliza,
And undo thy chamber door;
I can name the name of Jesus,
As I once could do before.'

Up then rose the sweet Eliza,—
Up she rose, and twirl'd the pin.
Straight the chamber door flew open,
And the dead man glided in.

With her comb she comb'd his ringlets,
For she felt but little fear:
On each lock that she adjusted
Fell a hot and briny tear.

'Listen, now, my good Sir Aager,
Dearest bridegroom, all I crave
Is to know how it goes with thee,
In that lonely place, the grave?'

'Every time that thou rejoicest,
And thy breast with pleasure heaves,
Then that moment is my coffin
Lin'd with rose and laurel leaves.

'Every time that thou art shedding
From thine eyes the briny flood,
Then that moment is my coffin
Fill'd with black and loathsome blood.

'Heard I not the red cock crowing,
Distant far upon the wind?
Down to dust the dead are going,
And I may not stop behind.

'Heaven's ruddy portals open,—
Daylight bursts upon my view;
Though the word be hard to utter,
I must bid thee, love, adieu!'

Up his mighty limbs he gather'd,
Took the coffin on his back,
To the church-yard straight he hasten'd
By the well-known, beaten, track.

Up then rose the sweet Eliza;
Tear-drops on her features stood,
While her lover she attended
Through the dark and dreary wood.

When they reach'd the lone enclosure,
(Last, sad, refuge of the dead)—
From the cheeks of good Sir Aager
All the lovely colour fled:

'Listen, now, my sweet Eliza,
If my peace be dear to thee:
Never, then, from this time forward,
Shed a single tear for me.

'Turn thy lovely eyes to heaven,
Where the stars are beaming pale;
Thou canst tell me, then, for certain,
If the night begins to fail.'

When she turn'd her eyes to heaven,
All with stars besprinkled o'er,
In the earth the dead man glided,
And she never saw him more.

Homeward went the sweet Eliza;
Oh, her heart was chill and cold:—
Wo is me! the Monday after,
Dead she lay beneath the mould!

SAINT OLUF.

FROM THE OLD DANISH.

St. Oluf was a mighty king,
Who rul'd the Northern land;
The holy Christian faith he preach'd,
And taught it, sword in hand.

St. Oluf built a lofty ship,
With sails of silk so fair;
'To Hornelummer I must go,
And see what 's passing there.'

'O do not go,' the seamen said,
'To yonder fatal ground,
Where savage Jutts,[1] and wicked elves,
And demon sprites, abound.'

St. Oluf climb'd the vessel's side;
His courage nought could tame!
'Heave up, heave up the anchor straight;
Let 's go in Jesu's name.

'The cross shall be my faulchion now—
The book of God my shield;
And, arm'd with them, I hope and trust
To make the demons yield.'

[1] Giants.—Jetté. *Dan.*

And swift, as eagle cleaves the sky,
The gallant vessel flew ;
Direct for Hornelummer's rock,
Through ocean's wavy blue.

'Twas early in the morning tide
When she cast anchor there ;
And, lo ! the Jutt stood on the cliff,
To breathe the morning air :

His eyes were like the burning beal—
His mouth was all awry ;
The truth I tell, and say he stood
Full twenty cubits high :

His beard was like a horse's mane,
And down his bosom roll'd ;
The claws that fenc'd his finger ends
Were frightful to behold.

' I never yet have seen,' he cried,
' A ship come near my strand,
That here to shore I could not drag,
By putting out my hand.'

The good St. Oluf smil'd thereat,
And thus address'd his crew :
' Now hold your tongues, and well observe
What I 'm about to do.'

The giant stretch'd his mighty arm ;
The ship was nigh his own ;
But when St. Oluf rais'd the cross,
He sank knee-deep in stone.

'Here am I, sunk knee-deep in stone!
My legs I cannot move;
But, since my back and fists are free,
My might thou yet shalt prove.'

'Be still, be still, thou noisy guest—
Be still for evermore;
Become a rock and beetle there,
Above the billows hoar.'

Up started then, from out the hill,
The demon's hoary wife;
She curs'd the king a thousand times,
And brandish'd high her knife.

Sore wonder'd then the little elves,
Who sat within the hill,
To see their mother, all at once,
Stand likewise stiff and still:

''Tis done,' they cried, 'by yonder wight,
Who rides upon the waves;
Let 's wade out to him, through the surf,
And beat him with our staves.'

At Hornelummer happen'd then,
What happen'd ne'er before;
The elfins wish'd to leave the hill,
And could not find a door:

They ran their heads against the wall,
And tried to break it through;
They could not break the solid rock,
But broke their necks in lieu.

Now, thanks to God, and Jesus Christ,
And good St. Oluf's arm,
To Hornelummer we can sail
Without mishap or harm.

THE HEROES OF DOVREFELD.

FROM THE OLD DANISH.

On Dovrefeld,[1] in Norway,
Were once together seen
The twelve heroic brothers
Of Ingeborg, the queen :

And they were all magicians,
Possest of mighty art,
Who freely read the Runic,
And knew the rhyme by heart.[2]

The first could turn the lightning,
And quench its ruddy gleam :
The second, with a whisper,
Could still the running stream :

The third beneath the water
Could dive like any fish :
The fourth could get provision
By striking on his dish :

The fifth upon the gold harp
So pleasantly could play,
That all the men who heard him
Began to dance away :

[1] Dovrefeld is the highest mountain in Norway, and in Europe.

[2] Some of the many powers attributed to 'Runic verses' will be found described in the song so intituled, in the latter part of this volume.

The sixth, he had a bugle,
And when he blew a blast,
The stoutest of his foemen
Would fly before him fast :

The seventh, unimpeded,
Through solid hills could roam :
The eighth could walk the ocean,
When billows were in foam :

The ninth could draw, by magic,
The fishes from the deep :
The tenth was never weary,
Nor overcome by sleep :

The eleventh bound the dragon
Which crept among the grass ;
And all he wish'd to happen
Was sure to come to pass :

The twelfth, who was reputed
The wisest of the band,
Knew what was going forward
In every foreign land.

And now, forsooth, I tell ye,
Who listen to my strain,
That such a set of brothers
Will ne'er be seen again.

SVEND VONVED.

FROM THE OLD DANISH.

Grimm, in the preface to his German translation of the Kiæmpé Viser, characterises this ballad in the following magnificent words :—

' Seltsam ist das Lied von dem Held Vonved. Unter dem Empfang des Zauberseegens und mit räthselhaften Worten, dass er nie wiederkehre oder dann den Tod seines Vaters rächen müsse, reitet er aus. Lange sieht er keine Stadt und keinen Menschen, dann, wer sich ihm entgegen stellt, den wirft er nieder, den Hirten legt er seine Räthsel vor über das edelste und abscheuungswürdigste, über den Gang der Sonne und die Ruhe des Todten : wer sie nicht löst, den erschlägt er ; trotzig sitzt er unter den Helden, ihre Anerbietungen gefallen ihm nicht, er reitet heim, erschlägt zwölf Zauberweiber, die ihm entgegen kommen, dann seine Mutter, endlich zernichtet er auch sein Saitenspiel, damit kein Wohllaut mehr den wilden Sinn besänftige. Es scheint dieses Lied vor allen in einer eigenen Bedeutung gedichtet, und den Mismuth eines zerstörten herumirrenden Gemüths anzuzeigen, das seine Räthsel will gelöst haben : es ist die Angst eines Menschen darin ausgedrückt, der die Flügel, die er fühlt, nicht frei bewegen kann, und der, wenn ihn diese Angst peinigt, gegen alles, auch gegen sein Liebstes, wüthen muss. Dieser Charakter scheint dem Norden gantz eigenthümlich ; in dem seltsamen Leben Königs Sigurd des Jerusalemfahrers, auch in Shakspeare's Hamlet ist etwas ähnliches.'

' Singular is the song of the hero Vonved. After having received the magic blessing, he rides out, darkly hinting that he must never return, or have avenged the death of his father. For a long time he sees no city and no man ; he then overthrows whomsoever opposes him ; he lays his enigmas before the herdsmen, concerning that which is most grand, and that which is most horrible ; concerning the course of the sun and the repose of the dead ; he who cannot explain them is slaughtered. Haughtily he sits among the heroes—their invitations do not please him—he rides home—slays twelve sorceresses who come against him—then his mother, and at last he demolishes his harp, so that no sweet sound shall in future soften his wild humour. This song, more than any of the rest, seems to be composed with a meaning of its own; and shows the melancholy of a ruined, wandering mind, which will have its enigmas cleared up! The anguish of a man is expressed therein, who cannot move freely the wings which he feels; and, who, when this anguish torments him, is forced to deal out destruction against all—even against his best-beloved. Such a character seems to be quite the property of the North. In the strange life of King Sigurd, the wanderer to Jerusalem, and likewise in Shakspeare's Hamlet, there is something similar.'

Svend Vonved sits in his lonely bower;
He strikes his harp with a hand of power;
His harp return'd a responsive din;
Then came his mother hurrying in:
  Look out, look out, Svend Vonved.

In came his mother Adeline,
And who was she, but a queen, so fine:
'Now hark, Svend Vonved! out must thou ride,
And wage stout battle with knights of pride.
  Look, out, look out, Svend Vonved.

'Avenge thy father's untimely end;
To me, or another, thy gold harp lend;
This moment boune [1] thee, and straight begone!
I rede [2] thee, do it, my own dear son.'
  Look out, look out, Svend Vonved.

Svend Vonved binds his sword to his side;
He fain will battle with knights of pride.
'When may I look for thee once more here?
When roast the heifer, and spice the beer?'
  Look out, look out, Svend Vonved.

[1] Boune, to get ready. [2] Rede, advise. Raader.—*Dan.*

'When stones shall take, of themselves, a flight,
And ravens' feathers are woxen [1] white,
Then may'st thou expect Svend Vonved home:
In all my days, I will never come.'
Look out, look out, Svend Vonved.

His mother took that in evil part:
'I hear, young gallant, that mad thou art;
Wherever thou goest, on land or sea,
Disgrace and shame shall attend on thee.'
Look out, look out, Svend Vonved.

He kiss'd her thrice, with his lips of fire:
'Appease, O mother, appease thine ire;
Ne'er wish me any mischance to know,
For thou canst not tell how far I may go.'
Look out, look out, Svend Vonved.

'Then I will bless thee, this very day;
Thou never shalt perish in any fray;
Success shall be in thy courser tall;
Success in thyself, which is best of all.
Look out, look out, Svend Vonved.

'Success in thy hand, success in thy foot,
In struggle with man, in battle with brute;
The holy God and Saint Drotten [2] dear
Shall guide and watch thee through thy career.
Look out, look out, Svend Vonved.

'They both shall take thee beneath their care,
Then surely thou never shalt evily fare:
See yonder sword of steel so white,
No helm nor shield shall resist its bite.'
Look out, look out, Svend Vonved.

[1] Woxen, grown. Voxen.—*Dan.*

[2] Jesus Christ.

Svend Vonved took up the word again—
'I 'll range the mountain, and rove the plain,
Peasant and noble I 'll wound and slay;
All, all, for my father's wrong shall pay.'
Look out, look out, Svend Vonved.

Svend Vonved bound his sword to his side,
He fain will battle with knights of pride;
So fierce and strange was his whole array,
No mortal ventur'd to cross his way.
Look out, look out, Svend Vonved.

His helm was blinking against the sun,
His spurs were clinking his heels upon,
His horse was springing, with bridle ringing,
While sat the warrior wildly singing.
Look out, look out, Svend Vonved.

He rode a day, he rode for three,
No town nor city he yet could see;
'Ha!' said the youth, 'by my father's hand,
There is no city in all this land.'
Look out, look out, Svend Vonved.

He rode and lilted, he rode and sang,
Then met he by chance Sir Thulé Vang;
Sir Thulé Vang, with his twelve sons bold,
All cas'd in iron, the bright and cold.
Look out, look out, Svend Vonved.

Svend Vonved took his sword from his side,
He fain would battle with knights so tried;
The proud Sir Thulé he first ran through,
And then, in succession, his sons he slew.
Look out, look out, Svend Vonved.

Svend Vonved binds his sword to his side,
It lists him farther to ride, to ride ;
He rode along by the grené shaw ; [1]
The Brute-carl [2] there with surprise he saw.
Look out, look out, Svend Vonved.

A wild swine sat on his shoulders broad,
Upon his bosom a black bear snor'd ;
And about his fingers, with hair o'erhung,
The squirrel sported, and weasel clung.
Look out, look out, Svend Vonved.

'Now, Brute-carl, yield thy booty to me,
Or I will take it by force from thee.
Say, wilt thou quickly thy beasts forego,
Or venture with me to bandy a blow ?'
Look out, look out, Svend Vonved.

'Much rather, much rather, I'll fight with thee,
Than thou my booty should'st get from me ;
I never was bidden the like to do,
Since good King Esmer in fight I slew.'
Look out, look out, Svend Vonved

'And did'st thou slay King Esmer fine ?
Why, then thou slewest dear father mine ;
And soon, full soon, shalt thou pay for him,
With the flesh hackt off from thy every limb !'
Look out, look out, Svend Vonved.

They drew a circle upon the sward ;
They both were dour, as the rocks are hard ;
Forsooth, I tell you, their hearts were steel'd,—
The one to the other no jot would yield.
Look out, look out, Svend Vonved.

[1] Grené shaw, green wood.—*Old English.*

[2] Brute-carl, dyre-carl.—*Original.*

They fought for a day,—they fought for two,—
And so on the third they were fain to do ;
But ere the fourth day reach'd the night,
The Brute-carl fell, and was slain outright.
  Look out, look out, Svend Vonved.

Svend Vonved binds his sword to his side,
Farther and farther he lists to ride :
He rode at the foot of a hill so steep,
There saw he a herd as he drove the sheep.
  Look out, look out, Svend Vonved.

'Now tell me, Herd, and tell me fair,
Whose are the sheep thou art driving there ?
And what is rounder than a wheel ?
And where do they eat the holiest meal ?'
  Look out, look out, Svend Vonved.

'Where does the fish stand up in the flood ?
And where is the bird that 's redder than blood ?
Where do they mingle the best, best, wine ?
And where with his knights does Vidrik dine ?'
  Look out, look out, Svend Vonved.

There sat the herd, he sat in thought ;
To ne'er a question he answer'd aught.
Svend gave him a stroke, a stroke so sore,
That his lung and his liver came out before.
  Look out, look out, Svend Vonved.

On, on went he, till more sheep he spied ;
The herd sat, too, by a deep pit's side.
'Now tell me, Herd, and tell me fair,
Whose are the sheep thou art tending there ?'
  Look out, look out, Svend Vonved.

'See yonder house, with turret and tower,
There feasting serves to beguile the hour;
There dwells a man, Tyggé Nold by name,
With his twelve fair sons, who are knights of fame.'
  Look out, look out, Svend Vonved.

'Enough, Sir Herd; now lend an ear—
Go, tell Tyggé Nold to come out here.'
From his breast Svend Vonved a gold ring drew;
At the foot of the herd the gold ring he threw.
  Look out, look out, Svend Vonved.

And as Svend Vonved approach'd the spot,
His booty among them they 'gan to allot.
Some would have his polish'd glaive,
Others, his harness, or courser brave.
  Look out, look out, Svend Vonved.

Svend Vonved stops, in reflection deep;
He thought it best he his horse should keep:
His hauberk and faulchion he will not lose,
Much rather to fight the youth will choose.
  Look out, look out, Svend Vonved.

'Had'st thou twelve sons to the twelve thou hast,
And cam'st in the midst of them charging me fast,
Sooner should'st thou wring water from steel,
Than thou in such fashion with me should'st deal.'
  Look out, look out, Svend Vonved.

He prick'd with his spur his courser tall,
Which sprang, at once, over the gate and wall.
Tyggé Nold there he has stretch'd in blood,
And his twelve sons too, that beside him stood.
  Look out, look out, Svend Vonved.

Then turn'd he his steed, in haste, about,—
Svend Vonved, the knight, so youthful and stout;
Forward he went o'er mountain and moor,
No mortal he met, which vex'd him sore.
  Look out, look out, Svend Vonved.

He came, at length, to another flock,
Where a herd sat combing his yellow lock:
'Now listen, Herd, with the fleecy care;
Listen, and give me answers fair.'
  Look out, look out, Svend Vonved.

'What is rounder than a wheel?
Where do they eat the holiest meal?
Where does the sun go down to his seat?
And where do they lay the dead man's feet?
  Look out, look out, Svend Vonved.

'What fills the valleys one and all?
What is cloth'd best in the monarch's hall?
What cries more loud than cranes can cry?
And what can in whiteness the swan outvie?
  Look out, look out, Svend Vonved.

'Who on his back his beard does wear?
Who 'neath his chin his nose does bear?
What 's more black than the blackest sloe?
And what is swifter than a roe?
  Look out, look out, Svend Vonved.

'Where is the bridge that is most broad?
What is, by man, the most abhorr'd?
Where leads, where leads, the highest road up?
And say, where the hottest of drink they sup.'
  Look out, look out, Svend Vonved.

The sun is rounder than a wheel.
They eat at the altar the holiest meal.
The sun in the West goes down to his seat :
And they lay to the East the dead man's
feet.
Look out, look out, Svend Vonved.

' Snow fills the valleys, one and all.
Man is cloth'd best in the monarch's hall.
Thunder cries louder than cranes can cry.
Angels in whiteness the swan outvie.
Look out, look out, Svend Vonved.

' His beard on his back the lapwing wears.
His nose 'neath his chin the elfin bears.[1]
More black is sin than the blackest sloe :
And thought is swifter than any roe.
Look out, look out, Svend Vonved.

' Ice is, of bridges, the bridge most broad.
The toad is, of all things, the most abhorr'd.
To paradise leads the highest road up :
And in hell the hottest of drink they sup.'
Look out, look out, Svend Vonved.

' Now hast thou given me answers fair,
To each and all of my questions rare ;
And now, I pray thee, be my guide,
To the nearest spot where warriors bide.'
Look out, look out, Svend Vonved.

[1] By this nose under the chin must be understood, that the elf has so long and crooked a nose, that it reaches and turns up under his chin. Crooked noses are, in all stories, allowed to be an ingredient of fiendish physiognomy.

'To Sonderborg I 'll show thee straight,
Where drink the heroes early and late:
There thou wilt find of knights a crew,
Haughty of heart, and hard to subdue.'
  Look out, look out, Svend Vonved.

With a bright gold ring was his arm array'd,
Full fifteen pounds that gold ring weigh'd,
That has he given the herd, for a meed,
Because he will show him the knights with speed.
  Look out, look out, Svend Vonved.

Svend Vonved enter'd the castle yard;
There Randulph, wrapt in his skins,[1] kept guard:
'Ho! Caitiff, ho! with shield and brand,
What art thou doing in this my land?'
  Look out, look out, Svend Vonved.

'I will, I will, with my single hand,
Take from thee, Knave, the whole of thy land:
I will, I will, with my single toe,
Lay thee and each of thy castles low.'
  Look out, look out, Svend Vonved.

'Thou shalt not, with thy single hand,
Take from me, Hound, an inch of my land;
And far, far less, shalt thou, with thy toe,
Lay me or one of my castles low.
  Look out, look out, Svend Vonved.

'Thou shalt not e'er, with finger of thine,
Strike asunder one limb of mine;[2]
I am for thee too woxen and stark,
As thou, to thy cost, shalt quickly mark.'
  Look out, look out, Svend Vonved.

[1] Svobt udi maard.—*Original.* [2] Slaae mig et mit Ledemod sonder.

Svend Vonved unsheath'd his faulchion bright,
With haughty Randulph he fain will fight ;
Randulph he there has slain in his might,
And Strandulph too, with full good right.
  Look out, look out, Svend Vonved.

The rest against him came out pell-mell,
Then slew he Carl Egé, the fierce and fell :--
He slew the great, he slew the small ;
He slew till his foes were slaughter'd all.
  Look out, look out, Svend Vonved.

Svend Vonved binds his sword to his side,
It lists him farther to ride, to ride ;
He found upon the desolate wold
A burly [1] knight, of aspect bold.
  Look out, look out, Svend Vonved.

' Now tell me, Rider, noble and good,
Where does the fish stand up in the flood ?
Where do they mingle the best, best wine ?
And where with his knights does Vidrik dine ? '
  Look out, look out, Svend Vonved.

' The fish in the East stands up in the flood.
They drink in the North the wine so good.
In Halland's hall does Vidrik dine,
With his swains around, and his warriors fine.'
  Look out, look out, Svend Vonved.

From his breast Svend Vonved a gold ring drew ;
At the foot of the knight the gold ring he threw :
' Go ! say thou wert the very last man
Who gold from the hand of Svend Vonved wan.'
  Look out, look out, Svend Vonved.

[1] Burly, strong.

Svend Vonved came where the castle rose ;
He bade the watchmen the gate unclose :
As none of the watchmen obey'd his cry,
He sprang at once over the ramparts high.
  Look out, look out, Svend Vonved.

He tied his steed to a ring in the wall,
Then in he went to the wide stone hall ;
Down he sat at the head of the board,
To no one present he utter'd a word.
  Look out, look out, Svend Vonved.

He drank and he ate, he ate and he drank,
He ask'd no leave, and return'd no thank ;
'Ne'er have I been on Christian ground
Where so many curst tongues were clanging around.'
  Look out, look out, Svend Vonved.

King Vidrik spoke to good knights three :
'Go, bind that lowering swain for me ;
Should ye not bind the stranger guest,
Ye will not serve me as ye can best.'
  Look out, look out, Svend Vonved.

'Should'st thou send three, and twenty times three,
And come thyself to lay hold of me ;
The son of a dog thou wilt still remain,
And yet to bind me have tried in vain.
  Look out, look out, Svend Vonved.

'Esmer, my father, who lies on his bier,
And proud Adeline, my mother so dear,
Oft and strictly have caution'd me
To waste no breath upon hounds like thee.'
  Look out, look out, Svend Vonved.

'And was King Esmer thy father's name,
And Adeline that of his virtuous Dame ?
Thou art Svend Vonved, the stripling wild,
My own dear sister's only child.
  Look out, look out, Svend Vonved.

'Svend Vonved, wilt thou bide with me here ?
Honour awaits thee, and costly cheer ;
Whenever it lists thee abroad to wend,
Upon thee shall knights and swains attend.
  Look out, look out, Svend Vonved.

'Silver and gold thou never shalt lack,
Or helm to thy head, or mail to thy back ;'
But to this and the like he would lend no ear,
And home to his mother he now will steer.
  Look out, look out, Svend Vonved.

Svend Vonved gallop'd along the way ;
To fancies dark was his mind a prey :
Riding he enter'd the castle yard
Where stood twelve witches wrinkled and scarr'd :
  Look out, look out, Svend Vonved.

There stood they all, with spindle and rok,[1]—
Each over the shinbone gave him a knock :
Svend turn'd his steed, in fury, round ;
The witches he there has hew'd to the ground.
  Look out, look out, Svend Vonved.

[1] Rok og teen. The Rok is no longer used in England, though still common in the North. It is a hazel stick, more than a yard long, round which the wool is wound. It is affixed to the side of the spinner, under the left arm.

He hew'd the witches limb from limb,
So little mercy they got from him ;
His mother came out, and was serv'd the same,
Into fifteen pieces he hackt her frame.
  Look out, look out, Svend Vonved.

Then in he went to his lonely bower,
There drank he the wine, the wine of power :
His much-lov'd harp he play'd upon
Till the strings were broken, every one.
  Look out, look out, Svend Vonved.

ROMANTIC BALLADS

THE TOURNAMENT.

FROM THE OLD DANISH.

This is one of those Ballads which, from the days of Arild, have been much sung in Denmark : we find in it the names and bearings of most of those renowned heroes, who are mentioned separately in other poems. It divides itself into two parts ;—the first, which treats of the warrior's bearings, has a great resemblance to the 178th chapter of the Vilkina Saga, as likewise has the last part, wherein the Duel is described, to the 180th and 181st chapters of the same.

I cannot here forbear quoting and translating what Anders Sorensen Vedel, the good old Editor of the first Edition of the Kiæmpe Viser, which appeared in 1591, says concerning the apparently superhuman performances of the heroes therein celebrated.

'Hvad ellers Kiæmpernes Storlemhed Styrke og anden Vilkaar berörer, som overgaaer de Menneskers der nu leve deres Væxt og Kraft, det Stykke kan ikke her noksom nu forhandles, men skal i den Danske Krönikes tredie Bog videligere omtales. Thi det jo i Sandhed befindes og bevises af adskillige Documenter og Kundskab, at disse gamle Hellede, som de kaldes, have levet fast længer, og været mandeligere större stærkere og höiere end den gemene Mand er, som nu lever paa denne Dag.'

'That part which relates to these Warriors' size, strength, or other qualities, so far surpassing the stature and powers of the men who now exist, cannot be here sufficiently treated upon, but shall be further discussed in the third Book of the Danish Chronicles : for, in truth, it is discovered and proved from various documents and sources, that these old heroes, as they are called, lived much longer, and were manlier, stouter, stronger, and taller, than man at the present day.'

Six score there were, six score and ten,
  From Hald that rode that day ;
And when they came to Brattingsborg
  They pitch'd their pavilion gay.

King Nilaus stood on the turret's top,
  Had all around in sight :
' Why hold those heroes their lives so cheap,
  That it lists them here to fight ?

' Now, hear me, Sivard Snaresvend ;
  Far hast thou rov'd, and wide,
Those warriors' weapons thou shalt prove,
  To their tent thou must straightway ride.'

It was Sivard Snaresvend,
  To the broad tent speeded he then :
' I greet ye fair, in my master's name,
  All, all, ye Dane king's men.

' Now, be not wroth that here I come ;
  I come as a warrior, free :
The battle together we soon will prove ;
  Let me your bearings see.'

There stands upon the first good shield
  A lion, so fierce and stark,
With a crown on his head, of the ruddy gold,
  That is King Diderik's mark.

There shine upon the second shield
  A hammer and pincers bright ;
Them carries Vidrik Verlandson,
  Ne'er gives he quarter in fight.

There shines upon the third good shield
  A falcon, blazing with gold ;
And that by Helled Hogan is borne ;
  No knight, than he, more bold.

There shines upon the fourth good shield
  An eagle, and that is red ;
Is borne by none but Olger, the Dane ;
  He strikes his foemen dead.

There shines upon the fifth good shield
  A couchant hawk, on a wall ;
That 's borne by Master Hildebrand ;
  He tries, with heroes, a fall.

And now comes forth the sixth good shield,
  A linden is thereupon ;
And that by young Sir Humble is borne,
  King Abelon's eldest son.

There shines upon the seventh good shield
  A spur, of a fashion so free ;
And that is borne by Hogan, the less,
  Because he will foremost be.

There shines upon the eighth good shield
  A gray wolf, meagre and gaunt ;
Is borne by youthful Ulf van Jern ;
  Beware how him you taunt !

There shine upon the ninth good shield
  Three arrows, and white are they ;
Are borne by Vidrik Stageson,
  And trust that gallant you may.

There shines upon the tenth good shield
  A fiddle, and 'neath it a bow ;
That 's borne by Folker Spillemand ;
  For drink he will sleep forego.

There shines upon the eleventh shield
A dragon that looks so dire ;
Is carried by Orm, the youthful swain ;
He trembles at no man's ire.

And, now, behold the twelfth good shield,
And upon it a burning brand ;
Is borne by stout Sir Vifferlin
Through many a prince's land.

There stands upon the thirteenth shield
A sprig of the mournful yew ;
That 's borne by Harrald Griskeson ;
And he 's a comrade true.

There stand upon the fourteenth shield
A cloak, and a mighty staff ;
And them bore Alsing, the stalwart monk,
When he beat his foes to chaff.

And now comes forth the fifteenth shield,
And upon it three naked blades
Are borne by good King Esmer's sons,
In their wars and furious raids.

There stands upon the sixteenth shield,
With coal-black pinion, a crow ;
That 's borne by rich Count Raadengaard ;
The dark Runes well can he throw.[1]

There shines upon the seventeenth shield
A horse, so stately and high,
Is borne by Count Sir Guncelin ;
'Slay ! slay ! bide not,' is his cry.

[1] By scattering 'Runes,' or Runic letters, over graves, provided they formed a particular rhyme, the ancient Scandinavians imagined that the dead might be aroused.

There shine upon the eighteenth shield
  A man, and a fierce wild boar,
Are borne by the Count of Lidebierg ;
  His blows fall heavy and sore.

There shines upon the nineteenth shield
  A hound, at the stretch of his speed ;
Is borne by Oisten Kiæmpe, bold ;
  He risks his neck without heed.

There shines upon the twentieth shield,
  Among branches, a rose, so gay ;
Wherever Sir Nordman comes in war,
  He bears bright honour away.

There shines on the one-and-twentieth shield
  A vase, and of copper 'tis made ;
That 's borne by Mogan Sir Olgerson ;
  He wins broad lands with his blade.

And now comes forth the next good shield,
  With a sun dispelling the mirk ;
And that by Asbiorn Mildé is borne ;
  He sets the knights' backs at work.[1]

There shines on the three-and-twentieth shield
  An arm, in a manacle bound ;
And that by Alvor Sir Langé is borne,
  To the heroes he hands mead round.

Now comes the four-and-twentieth shield,
  And a bright sword there you see ;
And that by Humble Sir Jerfing is borne ;
  Full worthy of that is he.

[1] Han lærer de Kiæmpers Ryg at verké.

There shines upon the next good shield
  A goss-hawk, striking his game;
That 's borne by a knight, the best of all—
  Sir Iver Blaa is his name.

Now comes the six-and-twentieth shield,
  A jav'lin there you spy;
Is borne by little Mimring Tan;
  From no one will he fly.

Such knights and bearings as were there,
  And who can them all relate;
It was Sivard, the Snaresvend;
  No longer he deign'd to wait.

'If there be one of the Dane king's men,
  Who at Dyst [1] is willing to ride,
Let him, I pray, without pause or delay,
  Meet me by the wild wood's side.

'The man among you, ye Danish court men,
  Who at Dyst has won most meeds;
Him I am ready to fight, this day,
  For both of our noble steeds.'

The heroes cast the die on the board;
  The die it roll'd so wide:
'Since, young Sir Humble, it stops by thee,
  'Gainst Sivard thou must ride.'

Sir Humble struck his hand on the board;
  No longer he lists to play:
I tell you, forsooth, that the rosy hue
  From his cheek fast faded away.

[1] To ride at Dyst, to battle on horseback.

'Now, hear me, Vidrik Verlandson;
  Thou art so free a man;
Do lend me Skimming, thy horse, this day;
  I 'll pledge for him what I can:

'Eight good castles, in Birting's land,
  As pledges for him I 'll set;
My sister too, the lily-cheek'd maid,
  A fairer thou ne'er hast met:

'Eight good castles, and eight good knights;
  I 'd scorn to offer thee less:
If Skimming should meet any hurt this day,
  My sister thou shalt caress.'

'If yonder mountains all were gold,
  And yonder streams were wine;
The whole for Skimming I would not take;
  I bless God he is mine.

'Sivard is a purblind swain;
  Sees not to his faulchion's end:
If Skimming were hurt thou couldst not pay me
  With the help of thy every friend.

'The sword it whirls in Sivard's hand,
  As whirl the sails of the mill;
If thou take Skimming 'gainst that wild fool,
  'Tis sorely against my will.'

Humble, he sat him on Skimming's back,
  So gallantly can he ride;
But Skimming thought it passing strange
  That a spur was clapt to his side.

The first course that together they rode,
So strong were the knightly two,
Asunder went Humble's saddle-ring,
And a furlong his good shield flew.

'Methinks thou art a fair young swain,
And well thy horse canst ride;
Dismount thee, straight, and gird up thy steed;
I am willing for thee to bide.'

The second course that together they rode
Was worthy of knights renown'd;
Then both their saddles burst in two,
And Humble was sent to the ground.

'Now have I cast thee from thy steed,
Thy courser by right is mine;
But, tell me, youthful and gallant swain,
Who art thou, and of what line?

'Now have I won from thee the prize,
And Skimming belongs to me;
But, tell me, youthful and gallant swain,
What parents gave birth to thee?'

'Abelon is my father's name;
He sits upon Birting's throne:
Queen Ellina my mother is,
And that for truth is known.

'Queen Ellina my mother is—
A Queen whom all admire;
Good King Abelon Haardestaal,
So call they my hoary sire.

'And who am I, but Humble, the young,
A knight of Birting's land;
Of hero race, whose fame extends
To the wide earth's farthest strand.'

'If Abelon be thy father's name,
The courser I straight restore;
Thou art, I find, my very good friend;
I knew thee not, youth, before.

'If Queen Ellina thy mother is,
Then Skimming thou hast rewon;
Thou art, indeed, my very good friend;
Thou art my sister's son.

'Take both the shield ropes, take them straight,
And bind me to yon oak tree;
Then hie thee back to King Diderik,
And say thou hast conquer'd me.'

In came Humble, the youthful knight,
Was clad in a kirtle, green;
'O! I have got my courser again,
And have bound the warrior keen.'

In came Humble, with boot and spur,
He cast on the table his sword:
'Sivard stands in the green wood bound,
He speaks not a single word.

'O, I have been to the wild forest,
And have seiz'd the warrior stark;
Sivard there was taken by me,
And tied to the oak's rough bark.'

'Now hear me, young Sir Humble, the knight,
'Tis plain a jest is meant,
Whenever Sivard was bound by thee,
'Twas done with his own consent.'

It was Vidrik Verlandson,
And he would fain know all.
'O, I will ride to the wood, and see
How Sivard endures his thrall.'

Vidrik spoke to his burly groom :
'Go, saddle me Skimming gray,
For I will ride to the wood, and hear
What Sivard himself will say.'

Sivard stands in the good green wood,
There sees he Vidrik ride :
'If Vidrik finds me bounden here,
He 'll hew my rib-bones from my side.'

Then loud laugh'd Vidrik Verlandson,
And Skimming began to neigh,
For Sivard rooted the oak tree up ;
He dar'd no longer stay.

The queen she sat in the high, high, loft,
And thence look'd far and wide :
'O there comes Sivard Snaresvend,
With a stately oak at his side.'

Then loud laugh'd fair Queen Gloriant,
As she look'd on Sivard full :
'Thou wert, no doubt, in great, great need,
When thou such flowers didst pull.'

The King he stood at the castle gate,
  In his robes and kingly crown :
' O there comes Sivard Snaresvend,
  And he brings us Summer to town.' [1]

Now dance the heroes by Brattingsborg ;
  They dance in their coats of felt ;
There dances Sivard, the purblind swain,
  With an oak tree under his belt.

[1] It was formerly the custom in Denmark, upon St. John's day, to celebrate the arrival of Summer, by troops of youths and maids going out into the woods, and thence returning bedecked with leaves and branches. This ceremony was called 'bringing Summer to town.'

VIDRIK VERLANDSON.

FROM THE OLD DANISH.

King Diderik sits in the halls of Bern,
  And he boasts of his deeds of might ;
So many a swain in battle he 's fell'd,
  And taken so many a knight.

King Diderik sits in the halls of Bern,
  And he strikes his moony shield ;
' O, would that I knew of a hero now,
  'Gainst whom I could take the field.'

Then answer'd Master Hildebrand,
  (For he knew all things best,)
' There sleeps a Giant at Birtingsberg ;
  Dar'st thou disturb his rest ? '

' Now, hear me, Master Hildebrand ;
  Thou art huge in body and limb ;
Thou foremost shall ride, in the wood, this day,
  And bear our challenge to him.'

Then answer'd Master Hildebrand,
  So careful a knight was he ;
' Not so, my Lord, will I do, this day,
  For the wages delight not me.'

Then out spoke Vidrik Verlandson,
  And he spoke in wrathful mood ;
' O, I 'll be first of the band, this day,
  All through the Birting wood.'

Then out spoke Vidrik Verlandson,
  And he spoke with lofty pride ;
' The smith he forg'd me a faulchion good,
  That can steel, like cloth, divide.'

They were three hundred valorous knights,
  Unto Birting's land that rode ;
They go in quest of Langben the Jutt,
  To the gloomy wood, his abode.

Then out spoke Vidrik Verlandson ;
  ' A wondrous game we 'll play ;
For I will ride in the green wood first,
  If ye 'll but trust me away.'

Then answer'd bold King Diderik,
  He answer'd hastily then ;
' When thou therein shalt have found the Jutt,
  Come back for me and my men.'

It was Vidrik Verlandson,
  In the forest alone he sped ;
And there he found so little a way,
  Which up to the Giant led.

It was Vidrik Verlandson,
  He came unto Birting's hill ;
There black and dread lay Langben the Jutt,
  He lay stretch'd out, and still.

It was Vidrik Verlandson,
With his lance touch'd him on the knee ;
'Wake up ! wake up ! now Langben the Jutt,
Thou sleepest full sound, I see.'

'Here have I lain, for many a year,
'Mid the leaf and the dew-wet herb ;
But never, till now, came a warrior by,
That has dar'd my sleep to disturb.'

'Here stand I, Vidrik Verlandson,
With a sword, so good, at my side ;
I came to wake thee up from thy sleep,
Betide whatever betide.'

It was Langben the Giant, then,
Turn'd up the white of his eye ;
'O, whence can come this warrior youth,
Who such bold words lets fly ?

'But hear, but hear, thou warrior youth ;
I will not do battle with thee,
Except thou prove of a knightly race ;
So thy lineage tell to me.'

'A handsome smith my father was,
And Verland hight was he :
Bodild they call'd my mother fair ;
Queen over countries three :

'Skimming I call my noble steed,
Begot from the wild sea-mare :
Blank [1] do I call my haughty helm,
Because it glitters so fair :

[1] Blank, clear, shining.—*Dan.*

‘ Skrepping I call my good thick shield ;
  Steel shafts have furrow’d it o’er :
Mimmering have I nam’d my sword ;
  ’Tis harden’d in heroes’ gore :

‘ And I am Vidrik Verlandson ;
  For clothes bright iron I wear :
Stand’st thou not up on thy long, long legs,
  I ’ll pin thee down to thy lair :

‘ Do thou stand up on thy long, long legs,
  Nor look so dogged and grim ;
The King holds out before the wood ;
  Thou shalt yield thy treasure to him.’

‘ All, all the gold that I possess,
  I will keep with great renown ;
I ’ll yield it at no little horse-boy’s word,
  To the best king wearing a crown.’

‘ So young and little as here I seem,
  Thou shalt find me prompt in a fray ;
I ’ll hew the head from thy shoulders off,
  And thy much gold bear away.’

It was Langben the mighty Jutt,
  With fury his heart was fir’d ;
‘ Ride hence! ride hence! thou warrior youth,
  If of life thou be not tir’d.’

Skimming sprang up, with both his legs,
  Against the giant’s side ;
Asunder went five of his rib-bones then,
  And the fight began at that tide.

It was Langben the lofty Jutt,
He wav'd his steel mace round ;
He sent a blow after Vidrik ;
But the mace struck deep in the ground.

It was Langben the lofty Jutt,
Who had thought his foeman to slay,
But the blow fell short of Vidrik ;
For the good horse bore him away.

It was Langben the lofty Jutt,
That shouted in wild despair :
' Now lies my mace in the hillock fast,
As though 'twere hammer'd in there ! '

Vidrik paus'd no moment's space ;
So ready was he to assail :
' Upon him, Skimming, upon him once more !
Now, Mimmering, now prevail ! '

He seiz'd his sword in both his hands,
Unto Langben Giant he flew ;
He struck him so hard in the hairy breast,
That the point his lungs went through.

Now Langben Giant has got a wound,
And he 's waken'd thoroughly now ;
So gladly would he have paid it back,
But, alas ! he knew not how.

' Accursed be thou, young Vidrik !
And accurs'd thy piercing steel !
Thou hast given me, see, a wound in my breast,
Whence rise the pains I feel.'

'I 'll hew thee, Giant, I 'll hew thee as small
As leaves that are borne on the blast,
Except thou showest me all the gear,
That hid in the forest thou hast.'

'Forbear, O Vidrik Verlandson,
Strike me not cruelly dead!
And I will lead thee straight to my house,
That 's thatch'd with gold so red.'

Vidrik rode, and the Giant crept,
So far through the forest ways,
They found the house with the red gold thatch'd;
It glitter'd like straw in a blaze.

'Therein, therein are heaps of gold,
No King has a greater store;
Do thou remove the big black stone,
And lift from the hinges the door.'

With both hands Vidrik seiz'd the stone,
But to stir it in vain did he try;
The Giant took it with finger and thumb,
And lifted it up in the sky.

'Now hear, now hear, thou warrior youth,
Thou canst wheel thy courser about;
But in every feat of manly strength
I could beat thee out and out.'

Then answer'd Vidrik Verlandson,
(He fear'd for himself some ill)
''Tis not the custom of any wise man
His strength on a stone to spill.'

'Therein, therein is much more gold
  Than fifteen kings can show;
Hear me, Vidrik Verlandson,
  Thou therein first shalt go.'

Then answer'd Vidrik Verlandson,
  (For his cunning intent he saw)
'Thou shalt lead the way into thine own house,
  For that is warrior-law.'

It was Langben the Giant then,
  To the door he stoop'd down low:
It was Vidrik Verlandson
  Cleft off his head at a blow.

Away the quivering body he drew,
  And propp'd it against an oak;
Then back he rode the long, long way,
  He 's thought of a wondrous joke.

With giant's blood he besmear'd himself,
  And besmear'd his steed all o'er;
Then back he rides to King Diderik,
  Pretends to be wounded sore.

'Here bide ye in peace, my companions good,
  All under the grass-green hill;
Langben the Giant has smote me to day,
  I doubt I shall fare but ill.'

'If thou from the Giant hast got a blow,
  Thy life must be nigh its close;
We 'll ride swift back to the halls of Bern,
  No man more will we lose.'

'Now wend thee, bold King Diderik,
  Wend into the wood with me ;
And all the gold that the giant had,
  That will I show to thee.'

'If thou hast slain the giant this day,
  'Twill far be blaz'd in the land ;
And the warrior lives not in this world,
  'Gainst whom thou may'st fear to stand.'

But what befel King Diderik's men ?
  When the giant they first perceiv'd,
They all stopp'd short, in the good green wood,
  Of courage at once bereav'd.

They thought the giant verily would
  That moment after them stride :
Not one of them all would have battled with him ;
  Back would they all have hied.

It was Vidrik Verlandson,
  He laugh'd at their craven fear :
'How would ye have fac'd him when alive,
  Ye dare not him, dead, go near ?'

With his lance's haft the body he push'd,
  The head came toppling down :
That the Giant was a warrior stark,
  Forsooth, I am forc'd to own.

Out took they then his ruddy gold,
  And shar'd it amongst the band :
To Vidrik came the largest part,
  For 'twas earn'd with his good hand.

Little car'd he for the booty, I ween,
But he thought of his meed of fame ;
When men should say, in the Danish land,
That the Giant he overcame.

So gladly rode they to Bern again ;
King Diderik gladdest of all :
There caus'd he Vidrik Verlandson
To sit next him in the hall.

ELVIR HILL.

FROM THE OLD DANISH.

Upon this Ballad Oehlenslæger founded his 'Elvir Shades,' a translation of which has already been given.

I RESTED my head upon Elvir Hill's side, and my
eyes were beginning to slumber;
That moment there rose up before me two maids,
whose charms would take ages to number.

One patted my face, and the other exclaim'd,
while loading my cheek with her kisses,
'Rise, rise, for to dance with you here we have
sped from the undermost caves and abysses.

'Rise, fair-headed swain, and refuse not to dance;
and I and my sister will sing thee
The loveliest ditties that ever were heard, and
the prettiest presents will bring thee.'

Then both of them sang so delightful a song, that
the boisterous river before us
Stood suddenly quiet and placid, as though 'twere
afraid to disturb the sweet chorus.

The boisterous stream stood suddenly still, though
accustom'd to foam and to bellow;
And, fearless, the trout play'd along with the pike,
and the pike play'd with him as his fellow.

The fishes, whose dwelling was deep in the flood,
up, up from their caverns did sally ;
The gay little birds of the forest began to warble,
forthwith, in the valley.

'Now, listen thou fair-headed swain, and if thou
wilt stand up and dance for a minute,
We 'll teach thee to open the sorcerer's book, and
to read all the Runic that 's in it.

'The bear and the wolf thou shalt trammel, unto
the thick stem of the oak, at thy pleasure ;
Before thee the dragon shall fly from his nest, and
shall leave thee sole lord of his treasure.'

Then about and around on the moonlight hill, in
their fairy fashion they sported,
While unmov'd sat the gallant and fair young
swain, whom they, in their wantonness,
courted.

'And wilt thou not grant us our civil request,
proud stripling, and wilt thou deny it ?
By hell's ruddy blazes, our gold-handled knife
shall lay thee for ever in quiet.'

And if my good luck had not manag'd it so, that
the cock crew out, then, in the distance,
I should have been murder'd by them, on the
hill, without power to offer resistance.

'Tis therefore I counsel each young Danish swain,
who may ride in the forest so dreary,
Ne'er to lay down upon lone Elvir Hill though he
chance to be ever so weary.

WALDEMAR'S CHASE.

The following Ballad is merely a versification of one of the many feats of Waldemar, the famed phantom hunter of the North, an account of whom, and of Palnatoka and Groon the Jutt, both spectres of a similar character, may be found in Thiele's Danské Folkesagn.

LATE at eve they were toiling on Harribee bank,
For in harvest men ne'er should be idle :
Towards them rode Waldemar, meagre and lank,
And he linger'd and drew up his bridle.

'Success to your labour ; and have ye to night
Seen any thing pass ye, while reaping ? '
'Yes, yes,' said a peasant, 'I saw something white,
Just now, through the corn-stubble creeping.'

'Which way did it go ? ' 'Why methought to the beach.'
Then off went Waldemar bounding ;
A few minutes after, they heard a faint screech,
And the horn of the hunter resounding.

Then back came he, laughing in horrible tone,
And the blood in their veins ran the colder,
When they saw that a fresh-slaughter'd mermaid was thrown
Athwart his proud barb's dappled shoulder.

Said he, 'I have chas'd her for seven score years,
As she landed to drink at the fountains.'
No more did he deign to their terrified ears,
But gallop'd away to the mountains.

THE MERMAN.

FROM THE OLD DANISH.

‘ Do thou, dear Mother, contrive amain
How Marsk Stig's daughter I may gain.’

She made him, of water, a noble steed,
Whose trappings were form'd from rush and reed.

To a young knight chang'd she then her son ;
To Mary's church at full speed he 's gone.

His foaming horse to the gate he bound,
And pac'd the church full three times round :

When in he walk'd with his plume on high,
The dead men gave from their tombs a sigh :

The priest heard that, and he clos'd his book ;
‘ Methinks yon knight has a strange wild look.’

Then laugh'd the maiden beneath her sleeve ;
‘ If he were my husband I should not grieve.’

He stepp'd over benches one and two :
‘ O, Marsk Stig's daughter, I doat on you.’

He stepp'd over benches two and three :
‘ O, Marsk Stig's daughter, come home with me.’

Then said the maid, without more ado,
'Here take my troth, I will go with you.'

They went from the church a bridal train,
And danc'd so gaily across the plain;

They danc'd till they came to the strand, and then
They were forsaken by maids and men.

'Now, Marsk Stig's daughter, sit down and rest;
To build a boat I will do my best.'

He built a boat of the whitest sand,
And away they went from the smiling land;

But when they had cross'd the ninth green wave,
Down sunk the boat to the ocean cave!

I caution ye, maids, as well as I can,
Ne'er give your troth to an unknown man.

THE DECEIVED MERMAN.

FROM THE OLD DANISH.

Fair Agnes alone on the sea-shore stood,
Then rose a Merman from out the flood :

'Now, Agnes, hear what I say to thee,
Wilt thou my leman consent to be ?'

'O, freely that will I become,
If thou but take me beneath the foam.'

He stopp'd her ears, and he stopp'd her eyes,
And into the ocean he took his prize.

The Merman's leman was Agnes there,—
She bore him sons and daughters fair :

One day by the cradle she sat and sang,
Then heard she above how the church bells rang :

She went to the Merman, and kiss'd his brow ;
'Once more to church I would gladly go.'

'And thou to church once more shalt go,
But come to thy babes back here below.'

He flung his arm her body around,
And he lifted her up unto England's ground.

Fair Agnes in at the church door stepp'd,
Behind her mother, who sorely wept.

'O Agnes, Agnes, daughter dear!
Where hast thou been this many a year?'

'O, I have been deep, deep under the sea,
And liv'd with the Merman in love and glee.'

'And what for thy honour did he give thee,
When he made thee his leman beneath the sea?'

'He gave me silver, he gave me gold,
And sprigs of coral my hair to hold.'

The Merman up to the church door came;
His eyes they shone like a yellow flame;

His face was white, and his beard was green—
A fairer demon was never seen.

'Now, Agnes, Agnes, list to me,
Thy babes are longing so after thee.'

'I cannot come yet, here must I stay
Until the priest shall have said his say.'

And when the priest had said his say,
She thought with her mother at home she 'd stay.

'O Agnes, Agnes, list to me,
Thy babes are sorrowing after thee.'

'Let them sorrow, and sorrow their fill,
But back to them never return I will.'

'Think on them, Agnes, think on them all;
Think on the great one, think on the small.'

'Little, O little, care I for them all,
Or for the great one, or for the small.'

O, bitterly then did the Merman weep;
He hied him back to the foamy deep:

But, often his shrieks and mournful cries,
At midnight's hour, from thence arise.

MISCELLANIES.

CANTATA.

THIS is Denmark's holyday ;
Dance, ye maidens !
Sing, ye men !
Tune, ye harpers !
Blush, ye heroes !
This is Denmark's holyday.

ONE VOICE.

In right's enjoyment, in the arm of love,
Beneath the olive's shadow,
The Daneman sat ;
Whilst wet and steaming wav'd the bloody flag
Above the regions of the sunny South.
Pure was our heaven,—
Pure and blue ;
For, with his pinions, angel Peace dispell'd
All reek and vapour from mild virtue's sphere ;
Then lower'd Battle's blood-bespatter'd son
Upon our coast,—
And haggard Envy lent to him her torch,
Which sparkled high with hell's sulphureous light,
Then fled the genius of peace, and wept

A SECOND VOICE.

But mighty thunders peal'd ; the earth it shook,
While rattled all the moss-grown giant stones,[1]
And Oldom's sunken grave-hill rais'd itself ;
Then started Skiold and Frodé,
And Svend, and Knud, and Waldemar,[2]
In copper hauberks up, and pointing to
Rust-spots of blood on faulchion and on shield—
They vanish'd :
And in the Gothic aisles, high arch'd and dim,
Wild flutter'd of itself, the ancient banner
Which hung above a hero's bones ;
The faulchion clatter'd loud and ceaselessly
Within the tomb of Christian the Fourth,[3]
By Tordenskiold's [4] chapel on the strand,
Wild rose the daring Mermaid's witching song ;

[1] Called in Danish Kiæmpe-steene ; these stones either mark the burial place of a warrior, or the spot where some very remarkable circumstance has occurred.

[2] These were ancient Danish monarchs renowned in song and tale, for warlike exploits and strange adventures. Not far from the Bridge of Væré in the diocese of Roeskild is King Frode's grave-hill, which, according to tradition, contains immense treasures, and is the richest in all the land. 'Around the King's neck is a gold chain, so long that its other end reaches round his feet.' *See Thiele's Danské Folkesagn.*

[3] Denmark's wisest and greatest king. He entertained a warm friendship for James the First of England, and, attended by his court, came to London to visit him. The ceremonies and rejoicings which this event gave rise to, are well described in an old German book, at present in the British Museum.

[4] Tordenskiold Juul and Hvidtfeld—celebrated Danish admirals. The memory of Tordenskiold is sacred among the peasantry, on account of the victories obtained by him over the Swedes. It is reported of him in Jutland, that when the shot of the enemy was directed thick and fast against him, he would shake the leaden bullets from out the folds of his clothes.

The stones were loosen'd round about the grave
Where lay great Juul ;
And Hvidtfeld, clad in a transparent mist,
With smiles cherubic beaming on his face,
Stray'd, arm in arm, with his heroic brothers,
Along the deep.

CHORUS.

We felt the presence of one and all ;
The old flags wav'd in the arsenal,
A wondrous spirit went round, went round
The Northern ground.

ONE VOICE.

Then waken'd Thor,[1]
And drew around his loins the mighty belt
Of bear-sinews ;
With love fraternal harden'd he his shield,
With eager haste he sharp'd his blunted glaive,
And, with the iron of his hammer, touch'd
Each Dane's and every Norman's breast—
Shot his heroic flame therein, and smil'd !

MANY VOICES.

And Denmark and Norway smil'd.

LOUD CHORUS.

Upon the water,
Upon the land,
We boun'd for slaughter,
At Thor's command.

[1] In the Northern mythology, the God of war and strength. He is girded by a belt of bear-sinews, and bears a hammer called 'Miolner,' which means the shatterer, and with which he destroys giants, demons, and other foes of Odin the supreme God.

MAIDENS.

Then fell our tears so quickly,
We breath'd, we breath'd so thickly,
While scarce our lips could stammer forth
Prayers for you, and for the North.

MATRONS.

And we, and we, with breasts that smarted,
  Knelt, lowly knelt, whilst firm ye stood,
From us and from affection parted,
  In reek and smoke, in brothers' blood !

CHORUS OF MEN.

Tenderness comes from God ;
  Woman and man in its praise should sing ;
But tenderness flies at honour's nod ;
  We offer all up to our land and King.

ONE VOICE.

What sang ye, warlike throngs ?
  Repeat, repeat this day,
One of the simple, nervous, songs
Ye murmur'd out, when, hot with wrongs,
  Ye waited the coming fray.

UNIVERSAL CHORUS.

We love, we all love thee, beneficent Peace, etc.

SOLO.

Like the wave of the wild North main,
Foaming and frothing came on our foe ;
Proud of his triumphs, proud of his train,
He thought to lay us low :

But, from Denmark's lines of oak,
A horrible, horrible volley outbroke;
Then tumbled his mast,
His courage fell fast;
And the wave, which resembled his furious mood,
Was now with his blood embrued.

CHORUS.

This is Denmark's holyday;
Dance, ye maidens!
Sing, ye men!
Tune, ye harpers!
Blush, ye heroes!
This is Denmark's holyday.

A VOICE.

But, hark! what sobbing and what mournful notes
Are mixing with our hymns of ardent joy!
Hush, hush, be still;
A band of white-rob'd maids approaches slow,
With lily chaplets round their yellow locks,
With heavy tear-drops in their sunken eye;
Broken and trembling sounds
The melancholy song,
Accompanied by harp-tones rising mild.

YOUTHFUL MAIDENS.

Love, with rosy fetter,
Held us firmly bound;
Pure unmix'd enjoyment
Grateful here we found.

Bosom, bosom meeting,
'Gainst our youths we press'd ;
Bright the moon arose, then,
Glad to see us blest.

Denmark's honour beckon'd,
Loud the cannon roar'd ;
Perish'd in the battle
They whom we ador'd.
Sweet is, grave, thy slumber,
Free from care and noise ;
Short are earthly sorrows,—
Endless heaven's joys.

SUDDEN CHORUS OF THE SLAIN WARRIORS IS HEARD FROM ON HIGH.

From the heavenly, clear, invisible, home
Our voices come :
No joy can resemble the joy which reigns
In our seraph veins.
Lov'd ones, lov'd ones, weep for us not,
Soon shall ye here partake of our lot ;
High o'er the stars' extremest line
The sun of affection more bright shall shine :
Brothers, brothers, 'tis sweet to die
For the land of our birth, and the maid of our eye.
Blest are ye who like us shall fall ;
The righteous Jehovah rewards, above,
Courage and love :
Hallelujah, peace be with you all !

MISCELLANIES

THE HAIL-STORM.

FROM THE NORSE.

Sigvald Jarl was a famous Sea Rover, who, when unengaged in his predatory expeditions, resided at Jomsborg, in Denmark. He was the terror of the Norwegian coasts, which he ravaged and pillaged almost at his pleasure. Hacon Jarl, who at that time sat on the Norwegian throne, being informed that Sigvald meditated a grand descent, and knowing that he himself was unable to oppose him, had recourse to his God, Thorgerd, to whom he sacrificed his son Erling. In what manner Thorgerd assisted him and his forces, when the Danes landed, will best be learned from the bold song which the circumstance gave rise to, and which the following is a feeble attempt to translate.

WHEN from our ships we bounded,
I heard, with fear astounded,
The storm of Thorgerd's waking,
From Northern vapours breaking;
With flinty masses blended,
Gigantic hail descended,
And thick and fiercely rattled
Against us there embattled.

To aid the hostile maces,
It drifted in our faces;
It drifted, dealing slaughter,
And blood ran out like water—
Ran reeking, red, and horrid,
From batter'd cheek and forehead;
We plied our swords, but no men
Can stand 'gainst hail and foemen.

And demon Thorgerd raging
To see us still engaging,
Shot, downward from the heaven,
His shafts of flaming levin;
Then sank our brave in numbers,
To cold eternal slumbers;
There lay the good and gallant,
Renown'd for warlike talent.

Our captain, this perceiving,
The signal made for leaving,
And with his ship departed,
Downcast and broken-hearted;
War, death, and consternation,
Pursu'd our embarkation;
We did our best, but no men
Can stand 'gainst hail and foemen.

THE ELDER-WITCH.

According to the Danish tradition, there is a female Elf in the elder tree, which she leaves every midnight ; and, having strolled among the fields, returns to it before morning.

THOUGH tall the oak, and firm its stem,
  Though far abroad its boughs are spread,
  Though high the poplar lifts its head,
I have no song for them.
  A theme more bright, more bright would be
  The winsome, winsome elder tree,
Beneath whose shade I sit reclin'd ;—
  It holds a witch within its bark,
  A lovely witch who haunts the dark,
And fills with love my mind.

When ghosts, at midnight, leave their graves,
  And rous'd is every phantom thing ;
  When mermaids rise and sweetly sing
In concert with the waves ;
  When Palnatoka,[1] on his steed,
  Pursues the elves across the mead,
Or gallops, gallops o'er the sea,
  The witch within the elder's bark,
  The lovely witch who haunts the dark,
Comes out, comes out to me.

[1] See preface to 'Waldemar's Chase,' p. 115.

Of leaves the fairies make our bed ;
  The knight, who moulders 'neath the elm,[1]
  Starts up with spear and rusted helm,—
By him the grace is said ;
  And though her kiss is cold at times,
  And does not scent of earthly climes,
Though glaring is her eye, yet still
  The witch within the elder's bark,
  The lovely witch who haunts the dark,
I prize, and ever will.

Yet, once I lov'd a mortal maid,
  And gaz'd, enraptur'd, on her charms,
  Oft circled in each other's arms,
Together, here we stray'd ;—
  But, soon, she found a fairer youth,
  And I a fairer maid, forsooth !
And one more true, more true to me,
  The witch within the elder's bark,
  The lovely witch who haunts the dark,
Has been more true to me.

[1] It was frequently the practice of the ancient Norsemen, after having entombed their dead kings and heroes, to plant oaks or other trees over them, in order to prevent their remains being disturbed with facility. In that sublimest of all poems, 'The Incantation of Hervor,' is a passage to the following effect :

> Hervadr, Hiorvadr, Hrani and Angantyr,
> I wake ye all under the roots of the trees.

MISCELLANIES

ODE.

FROM THE GÆLIC.

'Is luaimnach mo chodal an nochd.'

OH restless, to night, are my slumbers ;
Life yet I retain, but not gladness ;
My heart in my bosom is wither'd,
And sorrow sits heavy upon me.
For cold, in her grave-hill, is lying
The maid whom I gaz'd on, so fondly,
Whose teeth were like chalk from the quarry,
Whose voice was more sweet than harp music.
Like foam that subsides on the water,
Just where the wild swan has been playing ;
Like snow, by the sunny beam melted,
My love, thou wert gone on a sudden.
Salt tears I let fall in abundance,
When memory bringeth before me
That eye, like the placid blue heaven ;
That cheek, like the rose in its glory.
Sweet object of warmest affection,
Why could not thy beauty protect thee ?
Why, sparing so many a thistle,
Did Death cut so lovely a blossom ?
Here pine I, forlorn and abandon'd,
Where once I was cheerful and merry :

No joy shall e'er shine on my visage,
Until my last hour's arrival.
O, like the top grain on the corn-ear,
Or, like the young pine, 'mong the bushes;
Or, like the moon, 'mong the stars shining,
Wert thou, O my love, amongst women!

BEAR SONG.

FROM THE DANISH OF EVALD.

THE squirrel that 's sporting
Amid the green leaves,
Full oft, with its rustle,
The hunter deceives ;
Who starts—and believing
That booty is nigh,
His heart, for a moment,
With pleasure beats high.

' Now, courage ! ' he mutters,
And crouching below
A thunder-split linden,
He waits for his foe :
' Ha ! joy to the hunter ;
A monstrous bear
E'en now is approaching,
And bids me prepare.

' Hark ! hark ! for the monarch
Of forests, ere long,
Will breathe out his bellow,
Deep-throated and strong : '
Thus saying, he gazes
Intently around ;
But, death to his wishes !
Can hear not a sound :

Except when, at moments,
  The wind rising shrill
Wafts boughs from the bushes,
  Across the lone hill.
Wo worth, to thee, squirrel,
  Amid the green leaves,
Full oft thy loud rustle
  The hunter deceives.

NATIONAL SONG.

FROM THE DANISH OF EVALD.

KING Christian stood beside the mast;
Smoke, mixt with flame,
Hung o'er his guns, that rattled fast
Against the Gothmen, as they pass'd:
Then sunk each hostile sail and mast
In smoke and flame.
'Fly!' said the foe: 'fly! all that can,
Nor wage, with Denmark's Christian,
The dread, unequal game.'

Niels Juul look'd out, and loudly cried,
'Quick! now 's the time:'
He hoisted up his banner wide,
And fore and aft his foemen plied;
And loud above the battle cried,
'Quick! now 's the time.'
'Fly!' said the foe, ''tis Fortune's rule,
To deck the head of Denmark's Juul
With Glory's wreath sublime.'

Once, Baltic, when the musket's knell
Rang through the sky,
Down to thy bosom heroes fell
And gasp'd amid the stormy swell;
While, from the shore, a piercing yell
Rang through the sky!

'God aids me,' cried our Tordenskiold;
'Proud foes, ye are but vainly bold;
Strike, strike, to me, or fly!'

Thou Danish path to fame and might,
Dark-rolling wave,
Receive a friend who holds as light
The perils of the stormy fight;
Who braves, like thee, the tempest's might;
Dark rolling wave,
O swiftly bear my bark along,
Till, crown'd with conquest, lull'd with song,
I reach my bourne—the grave.

THE OLD OAK.

HERE have I stood, the pride of the park,
In winter with snow on my frozen bark;
In spring 'mong the flowers that smiling she spread,
And among my own leaves when summer was fled.
Three hundred years my top I have rais'd,
Three hundred years I have sadly gaz'd
O'er Nature's wide extended scene;
O'er rushing rivers and meadows green,
For though I was always willing to rove,
I never could yet my firm foot move.

They fell'd my brother, who stood by my side,
And flung out his arms so wide, so wide;
How envy I him, for how blest is he,
As the keel of a vessel he sails so free
Around the whole of the monstrous earth;
But I am still in the place of my birth.
I once was too haughty by far to complain,
But am become feeble through age and pain;
And therefore I often give vent to my woes,
When through my branches the wild wind blows.

A night like this, so calm and clear,
I have not seen for many a year;
The milk-white doe and her tender fawn
Are skipping about on the moonlight lawn;

And there, on the verge of my time-worn root,
Two lovers are seated, and both are mute:
Her arm encircles his youthful neck,
For none are present their love to check.
This night would almost my sad heart cheer,
Had I one hope or one single fear.

MISCELLANIES

LINES

TO SIX-FOOT THREE.

A LAD, who twenty tongues can talk,
And sixty miles a day can walk ;
Drink at a draught a pint of rum,
And then be neither sick nor dumb ;
Can tune a song, and make a verse,
And deeds of Northern kings rehearse :
Who never will forsake his friend,
While he his bony fist can bend ;
And, though averse to brawl and strife,
Will fight a Dutchman with a knife.
O that is just the lad for me,
And such is honest six-foot three.

A braver being ne'er had birth
Since God first kneaded man from earth :
O, I have cause to know him well,
As Ferroe's blacken'd rocks can tell.
Who was it did, at Suderöe,
The deed no other dar'd to do ?
Who was it, when the Boff [1] had burst,
And whelm'd me in its womb accurst—

[1] Between the islands of Ferroe the Sea exhibits a phenomenon, called, in the dialect of the Islanders, the Boff. Whilst the salt stream runs strong and glassy through its narrow channel, it is suddenly deformed by seven successive breakers, huge and foamy, which occur without any apparent cause, and infallibly overwhelm any boat which may chance to be in the way of their fury.

Who was it dash'd amid the wave,
With frantic zeal, my life to save?
Who was it flung the rope to me?
O, who, but honest six-foot three!

Who was it taught my willing tongue,
The songs that Braga [1] fram'd and sung?
Who was it op'd to me the store
Of dark unearthly Runic lore,
And taught me to beguile my time
With Denmark's aged and witching rhyme:
To rest in thought in Elvir shades,
And hear the song of fairy maids;
Or climb the top of Dovrefeld,
Where magic knights their muster held?
Who was it did all this for me?
O, who, but honest six-foot three!

Wherever fate shall bid me roam,
Far, far from social joy and home;
'Mid burning Afric's desert sands,
Or wild Kamschatka's frozen lands;
Bit by the poison-loaded breeze,
Or blasts which clog with ice the seas;
In lowly cot or lordly hall,
In beggar's rags or robes of pall,
'Mong robber-bands or honest men,
In crowded town or forest den,
I never will unmindful be
Of what I owe to six-foot three.

That form which moves with giant-grace;
That wild, though not unhandsome, face;

[1] The ancient Northern god of music and poetry.

That voice which sometimes in its tone
Is softer than the wood-dove's moan,
At others, louder than the storm
Which beats the side of old Cairn Gorm; [1]
That hand, as white as falling snow,
Which yet can fell the stoutest foe;
And, last of all, that noble heart,
Which ne'er from honour's path would start,
Shall never be forgot by me—
So farewell, honest six-foot three!

[1] A mountain in the Scottish Highlands.

NATURE'S TEMPERAMENTS.

FROM THE DANISH OF OEHLENSLÆGER.

SADNESS.

Lo, a pallid fleecy vapour
  Far along the East is spread ;
Every star has quench'd its taper,
  Lately glimmering over head.
On the leaves, that bend so lowly,
  Drops of crystal water gleam ;
Yawning wide, the peasant slowly
  Drives afield his sluggish team.
Dreary looks the forest, lacking
  Song of birds that slumber mute ;
No rough swain is yet attacking,
  With his bill, the beech's root.
Night's terrific ghostly hour
  Backward through time's circle flies ;
No shrill clock from moss-grown tower
  Bids the dead men wake and rise.
Wearied out with midnight riot
  Mystic Nature slumbers now ;
Mouldering bodies rest in quiet,
  'Neath their tomb-lids damp and low ;
Sad and chill the wind is sighing
  Through the reeds that skirt the pool,
All around looks dead or dying,
  Wrapt in sorrow, clad in dool.

GLEE.

Roseate colours on heaven's high arch
Are beginning to mix with the blue and the gray,
Sol now commences his wonderful march,
And the forests' wing'd denizens sing from the spray.
Gaily the rose
Is seen to unclose
Each of her leaves to the brightening ray.
Waves on the lake
Rise, sparkle, and break :
O Venus, O Venus, thy shrine is prepar'd,
Far down in the valley o'erhung by the grove ;
Where, all the day, Philomel warbles, unscar'd,
Her silver-ton'd ditty of pleasure and love.

Innocence smiling out-carrols the lark,
And the bosom of guilt becomes tranquil again ;
Nightmares and visions, the fiends of the dark,
Have abandon'd the blood and have flown from the brain.
Higher the sun
Up heaven has run,
Beaming so fierce that we feel him with pain ;
Man, herb, and flower,
Droop under his power.
O Venus, O Venus, thy shrine is prepar'd,
Far down in the valley o'erhung by the grove
Where, all the day, Philomel warbles, unscar'd,
Her silver-ton'd ditty of pleasure and love.

MADNESS.

What darkens, what darkens ?—'tis heaven's high roof :
What lightens ?—'tis Heckla's flame, shooting aloof :
The proud, the majestic, the rugged old Thor,
The mightiest giant the North ever saw,
Transform'd to a mountain, stands there in the field,
With ice for his corslet, and rock for his shield ;
With thunder for voice, and with fire for tongue,
He stands there, so frightful, with vapour o'er-hung.
On that other side of the boisterous sea
Black Vulcan, as haughty as ever was he,
Stands, chang'd to a mountain, call'd Etna by name,
Which belches continually oceans of flame.
Much blood have they spilt, and much harm have they done,
For both, when the ancient religions were gone,
Combin'd their wild strength to destroy the new race,
Who were boldly beginning their shrines to deface.
O, Jesus of Nazareth, draw forth the blade
Of vengeance, and speed to thy worshippers' aid ;
Beat down the old gods, cut asunder their mail—
Amen !—brother Christians, why look ye so pale.

THE VIOLET-GATHERER.

FROM THE DANISH OF OEHLENSLÆGER.

Pale the moon her light was shedding
  O'er the landscape far and wide;
Calmly bright, all ills undreading,
  Emma wander'd by my side.

Night's sad birds their harsh notes utter'd,
  Perching low among the trees;
Emma's milk-white kirtle flutter'd
  Graceful in the rising breeze:

Then, in sweetness more than mortal,
  Sang a voice a plaintive air,
As we pass'd the church's portal,
  Lo, a ghostly form stood there!

'Emma, come, thy mother 's calling;
  Lone I lie in night and gloom,
Whilst the sun and moon-beams, falling,
  Glance upon my marble tomb.'

Emma star'd upon the figure,—
  Wish'd to speak, but vainly tried,
Press'd my hand with loving vigour,
  Trembled—faulter'd—gasp'd—and died!

Home I bore my luckless maiden,
  Home I bore her in despair ;
Chilly blasts, with night-dew laden,
  Rustled through her streaming hair.

Plunging then amid the forest,
  Soon I found the stately tree,
Under which, when heat was sorest,
  She was wont to sit with me.

Down my cheek ran tears in fever,
  While with axe its stem I cut ;
Soon it fell, and I with lever
  Roll'd it straight to Emma's hut.

Kiss'd her oft, and love empassion'd
  Sung a song in wildest tones ;
While the oaken boards I fashion'd,
  Doom'd to hide her lovely bones.

Thereupon I sought the bower,
  Where she kept her single hive ;
Morning shone on tree and flower,
  All around me look'd alive.

Stung by bees in thousand places,
  Out I took the yellow comb ;
Emma, deck'd in all her graces,
  Past my vision seem'd to roam.

Soon of wax I form'd a taper,
  O'er my love it cast its ray,
'Till the night came, clad in vapour,
  When in grave I laid her clay.

Deep below me sank the coffin,
  While my tears fell fast as rain;
Deep it sank, and I, full often,
  Thought to heave it up again.

Soon as e'er the stars, so merry,
  Heaven's arch next night illum'd,
Sad I sought the cemetery,
  Where my true love lay entomb'd.

Then, in sweetness more than mortal,
  Sang a voice a plaintive lay;
Underneath the church's portal
  Emma stood in death array.

'Louis! come! thy love is calling;
  Lone I lie in night and gloom,
Whilst the sun and moon beams, falling,
  Glance upon my lowly tomb.'

'Emma! dear!' I cried in gladness,
  'Take me too beneath the sod;
Leave me not to pine in sadness,
  Here on earth's detested clod.'

'Death should only strike the hoary,
  Yet, my Louis, thou shalt die,
When the stars again in glory
  Shine upon the midnight sky.'

Tears bedeck'd her long eyelashes,
  While she kiss'd my features wan;
Then, like flame that dies o'er ashes,
  All at once the maid was gone.

Therefore, pluck I painted violets,
  Which shall strew my lifeless clay,
When, to night, the stars have call'd me
  Unto joys that last for aye.

ODE TO A MOUNTAIN-TORRENT.

FROM THE GERMAN OF STOLBERG.

How lovely art thou in thy tresses of foam,
And yet the warm blood in my bosom grows chill,
When yelling thou rollest thee down from thy home,
'Mid the boom of the echoing forest and hill.

The pine-trees are shaken—they yield to thy shocks,
And spread their vast ruin wide over the ground,
The rocks fly before thee—thou seizest the rocks,
And whirl'st them like pebbles contemptuously round.

The sun-beams have cloth'd thee in glorious dyes,
They streak with the tints of the heavenly bow
Those hovering columns of vapour that rise
Forth from the bubbling cauldron below.

But why art thou seeking the ocean's dark brine ?
If grandeur makes happiness, sure it is found,
When forth from the depths of the rock-girdled mine
Thou boundest, and all gives response to thy sound.

Beware thee, O torrent, of yonder dark sea,
For there thou must crouch beneath tyranny's rod,
Here thou art lonely, and lovely, and free,—
Loud as a thunder-peal, strong as a god.

True, it is pleasant, at eve or at noon,
To gaze on the sea and its far-winding bays,
When ting'd with the light of the wandering moon,
Or red with the gold of the midsummer rays.

But, torrent, what is it ? what is it ?—behold
That lustre as nought but a bait and a snare,
What is the summer sun's purple and gold
To him who breathes not in pure freedom the air.

Abandon, abandon, thy headlong career—
But downward thou rushest—my words are in vain,
Bethink thee that oft-changing winds domineer
On the billowy breast of the time-serving main.

Then haste not, O torrent, to yonder dark sea,
For there thou must crouch beneath tyranny's rod ;
Here thou art lonely, and lovely, and free,—
Loud as a thunder-peal, strong as a god.

RUNIC VERSES.

O THE force of Runic verses,
  O the mighty strength of song
Cannot baffle all the curses
  Which to mortal state belong.

Slaughter'd chiefs, that buried under
  Heaps of marble, long have lain,
Song can rend your tomb asunder,
  Give ye life and strength again.

When around his dying capture,
  Fierce, the serpent draws his fold,
Song can make him, wild with rapture,
  Straight uncoil, and bite the mould.

When from keep and battled tower,
  Flames to heaven upward strain,
Song has o'er them greater power,
  Than the vapours dropping rain.

It can quench the conflagration
  Striding o'er the works of art;
But nor song nor incantation
  Can appease love's cruel smart.

O the force of Runic verses,
  O the mighty strength of song
Cannot baffle all the curses
  Which to mortal state belong.

THOUGHTS ON DEATH.

FROM THE SWEDISH OF C. LOHMAN.

PERHAPS 'tis folly, but still I feel
My heart-strings quiver, my senses reel,
Thinking how like a fast stream we range
Nearer and nearer to yon dread change,
When soul and spirit filter away,
And leave nothing better than senseless clay.

Yield, beauty, yield ; for the grave does gape,
And horribly alter'd reflects thy shape,—
For ah ! think not those childish charms
Will rest unrifled in its cold arms,
And think not there, that the rose of love
Will bloom on thy features as here above.

Let him who roams at vanity fair,
In robes that rival the tulip's glare,
Think on the chaplet of leaves which round
His fading forehead will soon be bound ;
Think on each dirge the priests will say
When his cold corse is borne away.

Let him who seeketh for wealth uncheck'd
By fear of labour—let him reflect,
The gold he wins will brightly shine,
When he has perish'd with all his line.
Though man may rave and vainly boast,
We are but ashes when at the most.

MISCELLANIES

BIRDS OF PASSAGE.

FROM THE SWEDISH.

So hot shines the sun upon Nile's yellow stream,
That the palm-trees can save us no more from his beam;
Now comes the desire for home, in full force,
And Northward our phalanx bends swiftly its course.

Now dim underneath us, through distance we view
The green grassy earth, and the ocean's deep blue;
There tempests and frequent disasters arise,
Whilst free and untroubled we wend through the skies.

Lo, high among mountains a meadow lies spread,
And there we alight, and get ready our bed;
There hatch we our eggs, and beneath the chill pole
We wait while the summer months over us roll.

No hunter, desirous to make us his prey,
Invades our lone valley by night or by day;
But green-mantled fairies their merry routs hold,
And fearless the pigmy[1] there hammers its gold.

[1] The Duergar, or Dwarf-elves, of Scandinavia are famous for the dexterity with which they fabricate ornaments of every kind, from the gold which they dig out of the depths of the hills.

But when pallid winter, again on the rocks
  Shakes down in a shower the snow from his
    locks,
Then comes the desire for heat, in full force,
  And Southward our phalanx bends swiftly its
    course.

To the verdant Savannah, and palm-shaded plain,
  Where the Nile rolls his water, we hurry again ;
There rest we till summer's sun, waxing too hot,
  Makes us wish for our native, our hill-girded
    spot.

THE BROKEN HARP.

O THOU, who, 'mid the forest trees,
With thy harmonious trembling strain,
Could'st change at once to soothing ease,
My love-sick bosom's cruel pain :
Thou droop'st in dreary silence now,
With shiver'd frame, and broken string,
While here, unhelp'd, beneath the bough
I sit, and feebly strive to sing.

The moon no more illumes the ground ;
In night and vapour dies my lay ;
For with thy sweet and melting sound
Fled, all at once, her silver ray :
O soon, O soon, shall this sad heart,
Which beats so low, and bleeds so free,
O'ercome by its fell load of smart,
Be broke, O ruin'd harp, like thee !

SCENES.

OBSERVE ye not yon high cliff's brow,
Up which a wanderer clambers slow,
'Tis by a hoary ruin crown'd,
Which rocks when shrill winds whistle round;
That is an ancient knightly hold,—
Alas! it droops, deserted, cold;
And sad and cheerless seems to gaze,
Back, back, to yon heroic days,
When youthful Kemps,[1] completely arm'd,
And lovely maids around it swarm'd.
You, in the tower, a hole may see;
A window there has ceas'd to be.
From that once lean'd a damsel bright,
In evening's red and fading light,
And star'd intently down the way,
Up which should come her lover gay:
But, time it flies on rapid wing—
Far off a church is towering,
Within it stand two marble stones,
That rest above the lovers' bones.
But see, the wanderer, with pain,
Has reach'd the pile he wish'd to gain;
Whilst Sol, behind the ruin'd walls,
Down into sacred nature falls.

[1] Kemp, a warrior.—*Old Eng.* *Dan.* Kiempé.

See, there, two hostile nobles fight,
With tiger-rage and giant-might.
There 's seen no smoke, there 's heard no shot,
For guns and powder yet were not.
'Twas custom then, when foemen warr'd,
To win or lose with spear and sword :
A wild heroic song they yell,
And each the other seeks to fell.
Oft, oft, her ownself to destroy,
Her own hand nature does employ.
There casts the hill up fire-flakes,
And Earth's gigantic body quakes :
There, lightnings through the high blue flash,
And ocean's billows wildly dash :
There, men 'gainst men their muscles strain,
And deal out death, and wounds, and pain.
O Nature ! to thyself show less
Of hate, and more of tenderness.

How dusky is the air around ;
We are no more above the ground ;
But, down we wend within the hill,
Whose springs our ears with hissings fill.
See, there, how rich the ruddy gold
Winds snakeways, 'midst the clammy mould
And hard green stone. By torches' ray,
The harvest there men mow away.
But, see ye not yon gath'ring cloud,
Which 'gainst them cometh paley proud ;
That holds the spirit of the hill,
Who brings death in its hand so chill :
If down they do not quickly fall,
Most certainly 'twill slay them all ;

For sorely wrathful is its mood,
Because they break its solitude :
Because its treasure off they bear,
And fling light o'er its gloomy lair.
'Tis white, and Kobbold is the name
Which it from oldest days does claim.

Now, back at once into time we go,
For many a hundred years, I trow.
A gothic chamber salutes your sight :
A taper gleams feebly through the night ;
A ghostly man by the board you see,
With his hand to his temples muses he :
Parchments, with age discolour'd and dun ;
Ancient shields all written upon ;
Tree-bark, bearing ciphers half defac'd ;
Stones with Runes and characters grac'd ;
Things of more worth than ye are aware,
On the mighty table are pil'd up there.
He gazes now in exstatic trance
Through the casement, out into nature's expanse.
Whene'er we sit at the lone midnight,
And stare out into the dubious light,
Whilst the pallid moon is peering o'er
Ruin'd cloister and crumbling tower,
Feelings so wondrous strange come o'er us ;
The past, and the future, arise before us ;
The present fadeth, unmark'd, away
In the garb of insignificancy.
He gazes up into nature's height,
The noble man with his eye so bright ;
He gazes up to the starry skies,
Whither, sooner or later, we hope to rise ;

And now he takes in haste the pen,
And the spirit of Oldom flows from it amain;
The scatter'd Goth-songs he changes unto
An Epic which maketh each bosom to glow.
Thanks to the old Monk, toiling thus—
They call him Saxo Grammaticus.

An open field before you lies,
A wind-burst o'er its bosom sighs,
Now all is still, all seems asleep;
'Midst of the field there stands a heap,
Upon the heap stand Runic stones,
Thereunder rest gigantic bones.
From Arild's time, that heap stands there,
But now 'tis till'd with utmost care,
In order that its owner may
Thereoff reap golden corn one day.
Oft has he tried, the niggard soul,
The mighty stones away to roll,
As useless burdens of his ground;
But they for that too big were found.
See, see! the moon through cloud and rack
Looks down upon the letters black,
And when the ghost its form uprears
He shines upon its bursting tears—
For oh! the moon 's an ancient man,
Describe him, mortal tongue ne'er can,
He shines alike, serene and bright,
At midmost hour of witching night,
Upon the spot of love and glee,
And on the gloomy gallows-tree.
Upon each Rune behold him stare,
While off he hastes through fields of air;

He understands those signs, I 'll gage,
Whose meaning lies in sunken age;
And if he were in speaking state,
No doubt the old man could relate
Strange things that have on earth occurr'd,
Of which fame ne'er has said a word;
But since with look, with look alone,
He cannot those events make known,
He waketh from his height sublime
Mere longing for the dark gone time.

THE SUICIDE'S GRAVE.

FROM THE GERMAN.

This piece is not translated for the sentiments which it contains, but for its poetical beauties. Although the path of human life is rough and thorny, the mind may always receive consolation by looking forward to the world to come. The mind which rejects a future state has to thank itself for its utter misery and hopelessness.

THE evening shadows fall upon the grave
On which I sit ; it is no common heap,—
Below its turf are laid the bones of one,
Who, sick of life and misery, did quench
The vital spark which in his bosom burn'd.

The shadows deepen, and the ruddy tinge
Which lately flooded all the western sky
Has now diminish'd to a single streak,
And here I sit, alone, and listen to
The noise of forests, and the hum of groves.

This is the time to think of nature's God,
When birds and fountains, streams and woods,
  unite
Their various-sounding voices in his praise :
Shall man alone refuse to sing it—yes,
For man, alone, has nought to thank him for.

There 's not a joy he gives to us on earth
That is not dash'd with bitterness and gall,
Only when youth is past, and age comes on,
Do we find quiet—quiet is not bliss,
Then tell me, God, what I 've to thank thee for.

But to recur to him who rests beneath—
He had a heart enthusiastic, warm,
And form'd for love—no prejudice dwelt there ;
He roam'd about the world to find a heart
Which felt with his, he sought, and found it not.

Or if he found it, providence stepp'd in,
And tore the cherish'd object from his sight,
Or fill'd its mind with visions weak and vain—
Could he survive all this ? ah, no ! he died,—
Died by the hand which injur'd none but him.

And did he die unpitied and unwept,—
Most probably, for there are fools who think
'Tis crime in man to take what is his own—
And 'twas on account they laid him here,
Within this sweet, unconsecrated, spot.

There comes a troop of maidens and of youths
Home from their labour—hark ! they cease their song,
And, pointing to the grave, with trembling hands,
They make a circuit, thinking that in me
The ghost of the self-murderer they view—
Which, fame says, wanders here.

Date Due
